Audio Access Included

# FLUTE

BY JENNIFER CLIPPERT

# AEROBICS

A **50-WEEK** Workout Program for Developing, Improving, and Maintaining Flute Technique

## Contents

To access audio visit:
**www.halleonard.com/mylibrary**
Enter Code
8589-5528-3993-3616

Cover Illustration by Birck Cox

ISBN 978-1-4950-0960-0

## HAL•LEONARD®
## CORPORATION

7777 W. BLUEMOUND RD. P.O. BOX 13819 MILWAUKEE, WI 53213

In Australia Contact:
**Hal Leonard Australia Pty. Ltd.**
4 Lentara Court
Cheltenham, Victoria, 3192 Australia
Email: ausadmin@halleonard.com.au

Visit Hal Leonard Online at
**www.halleonard.com**

# INTRODUCTION

**F**lute Aerobics is arranged in weekly practice units of five separate categories: Tone, Scales, Finger Mobility, Articulation, and Flexibility. These are intended for daily concentrated practice on one area, allowing the remaining two days of the week for review of all the week's exercises. Advanced students may find it possible to cover the material in one day, with enough variations to last throughout the week. Here is a brief description of the five categories:

## Tone

Just as an athlete must warm up and stretch before running, a flutist needs to stretch before playing. These etudes should be done *very* slowly; often they become much more difficult at slower tempi. Pay attention to the smallest details: connection between notes, finger coordination, intonation, attacks, and releases. It's easy to become overwhelmed with the particulars, but that's okay. This is the time and place to be tone-obsessed.

## Scales

Scales are the foundation of everything we play. It is not possible to truly understand music until you grasp its underlying structure. Because of this, there is no such thing as too many scales. I've suggested very slow tempi for beginning these studies to allow for absolute rhythmic precision of finger changes. Everyone can play scales fast, but not everyone can play them fast and clean. Worry about the speed after you achieve solid technique.

## Finger Mobility

These short little exercises may look easy, but they often can take the bulk of your practice time. Be sure to repeat each measure at least four times, and be conscious of economical finger motion. Keep the fingers relaxed and close to the keys, wrists relaxed and open, and a good body position.

## Articulation

These are studies on the many different types of articulation. I've found these to be similar to the tone studies; they are frequently harder when they are slower. Work with your teacher to find the best tongue position and syllable, and be consistent.

## Flexibility

These are an extension of the tone and finger mobility exercises. Usually they're tone exercises that should be played more quickly, but the fingers must be absolutely precise. Save these for later in your practice session.

## HOW TO GET STARTED

Before beginning any practice, the first thing you should do is just play. Improvise a bit, keep it simple and easy, just to get everything moving. You want to practice with warm muscles, not cold ones. Take a few minutes to work on some breathing exercises. Make sure you are physically comfortable and have everything you need to succeed (stand, book, pencil, tuner, metronome, glass of water). I also recommend breaks after every 30 minutes of practice.

## SITTING OR STANDING?

There is much debate over whether we should practice sitting or standing. My answer? Both! I feel most at ease standing, yet most professional players find themselves sitting for ensemble performances. You must be equally comfortable. I find it easier to achieve optimum posture in students while standing, and we often breathe our best this way, too. If you choose to sit, make sure your sitting posture is just as good as your standing posture. Work with your teacher to find the best position for you.

## TO VIBRATE OR NOT TO VIBRATE...

...That is the question. When working on tone studies, I always begin without vibrato. If I'm going to eat cake, I want to make sure it doesn't just look pretty but that it tastes good, too! So when working on tone, make sure the cake (your tone) is as tasty as your frosting (your vibrato). Ultimately they blend together to form one beautiful sound, but I find it much easier to fix and perfect my sound without the vibrato on top. All these exercises can be played both ways to different benefits.

## SPEED DEMONS

Some of us like to play fast... I used to be one of those, too. And while I still do, there is much benefit to learning and playing something slowly before speeding off. Slow and steady with modest acceleration over time will help you retain technique the best.

## FINAL THOUGHTS

While the exercises in this book have been separated and distributed by day, I have found that the best results are achieved when you piggyback ideas. In other words, when you are playing scales, still be thinking about your tone. Scales with bad tone are just that—bad. If you play your scales with a beautiful tone, clear articulation, and solid fingers, you will retain much more of your hard work than if you compartmentalize your practice. Layer the concepts for greatest impact.

*–Jennifer Clippert*

## ABOUT THE ONLINE AUDIO

On the title page of this book you will find a code that allows you to access the online demo tracks. To hear a performance of a given etude, refer to its track number. You can listen to the demo tracks online or download them to your computer and/or mobile device.

# WEEK 1

## TONE

The foundation for a beautiful flute tone is built from the bottom up. Play the first note of this exercise with your most beautiful tone (repeat and restart as necessary), and match it seamlessly into the next note. The goal is to make the beauty of the last note match the quality of the first note. This should be played without vibrato to get to the core of your sound. Slower is better.

**Advanced tip:** Focus on the beginning of the note (matching articulation), the ends of each note (sustain, diminuendo or taper), add vibrato and practice with a tuner for consistent pitch throughout.

**TRACK 1**

## SCALES

Beginning with the basics: Focus on smooth, even fingers and build in speed as appropriate.

**Note:** Throughout the book, only the printed scales are included on the audio tracks (Track 2 presents the C major scale.) As a practice tool, all the major scales are presented below, in the Circle of Fourths. Feel free to dog-ear these pages for easy reference.

**Advanced tip:** Vary articulations to include the following:

**TRACK 2**

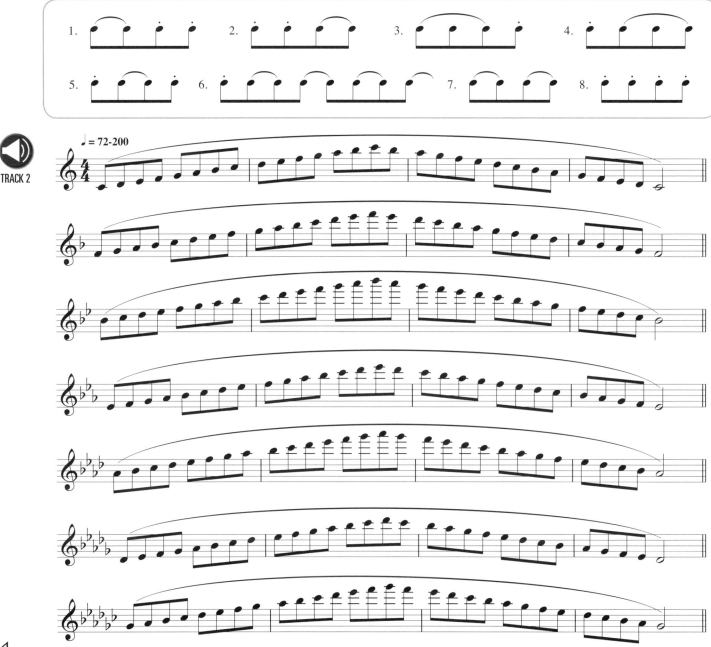

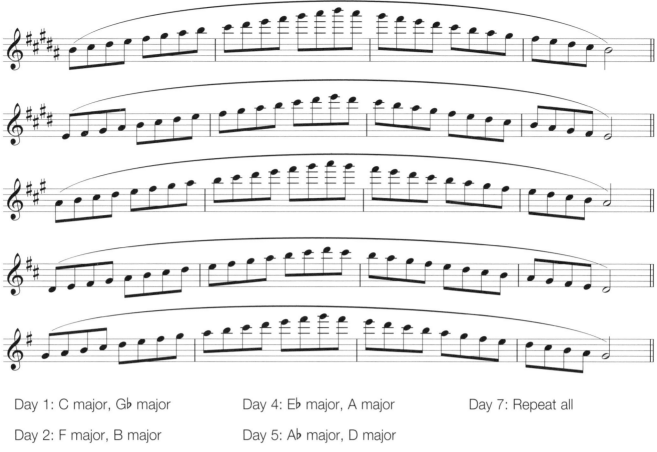

Day 1: C major, G♭ major    Day 4: E♭ major, A major    Day 7: Repeat all

Day 2: F major, B major     Day 5: A♭ major, D major

Day 3: B♭ major, E major    Day 6: D♭ major, G major

## FINGER MOBILITY

Strive for evenness of fingers. Repeat each measure four times, more if necessary. Increase speed with the metronome over time.

**Note:** Throughout the book, only the first four measures of the finger mobility exercises are included on the audio tracks.

TRACK 3

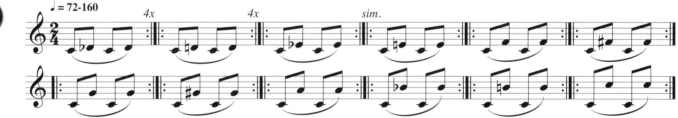

## ARTICULATION

Legato tonguing. Always strive for more tone, less tongue in your sound. Focus on the lightness and consistency of the articulation. Use the unarticulated notes ("hoh") to reinforce support. The following articulated noted ("doh") should be very light, serving only to articulate—not separate—the note.

TRACK 4

## FLEXIBILITY

Using the same concepts from the tone study, seamlessly blend one note into the next.

**Advanced tip:** Vary speed and dynamic, practice with a tuner. Work up to ♩ = 72.

TRACK 5

## TONE

Continue to focus on consistency of sound. Experiment with different vowel sounds as you ascend to find the most resonance. The goal is to have the first and last notes be equal in quality. Slower is better.

**Advanced tip:** Focus on the beginning of the note (matching articulation), the ends of each note (sustain, diminuendo or taper), add vibrato and practice with a tuner for consistent pitch throughout.

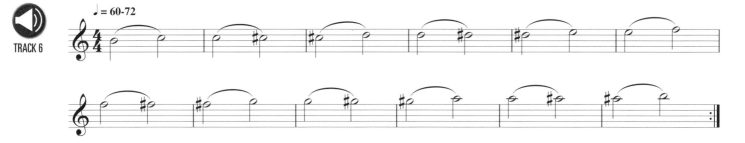

**TRACK 6**

## SCALES

Two-octave natural minor scales. Focus on smooth, even fingers. Build in speed as appropriate. (See Track 2 for audio example.)

**Advanced tip:** Vary articulations to include the following:

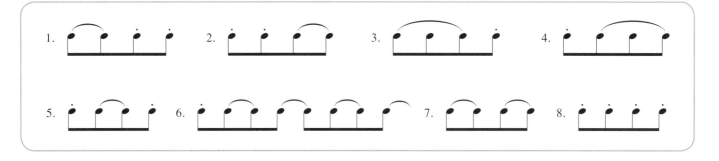

Day 1: A minor, E♭ minor

Day 2: D minor, G♯ minor

Day 3: G minor, C♯ minor

Day 4: C minor, F♯ minor

Day 5: F minor, B minor

Day 6: B♭ minor, E minor

Day 7: Repeat all

## FINGER MOBILITY

Strive for evenness of fingers. Repeat each measure four times, more if necessary. Increase speed with the metronome over time.

**TRACK 7**

## ARTICULATION

Play through the following exercise with legato tongue. Transpose through all major keys with the indicated starting pitch below.
**Note:** Track 8 demonstrates only the original.

**TRACK 8**

Transpose through all major keys, with beginning pitches:

## FLEXIBILITY

Using the same concepts from the tone study, seamlessly blend one note into the next.
**Advanced tip:** Vary speed and dynamic, practice with a tuner, and play ♩ = 60-72.

**TRACK 9**

## TONE

Continue to work on strengthening your tone from the bottom up. Work not only on matching tone quality throughout, but use increased support and lip pressure to increase the volume. Slower is better.

**Advanced tip:** Strive to play at six distinct volume levels: *pp*, *p*, *mp*, *mf*, *f*, *ff*.

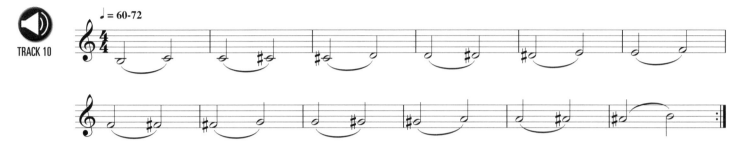

## SCALES

Two-octave harmonic minor scales. Focus on smooth, even fingers. Build in speed as appropriate. (See Track 2 for audio example.)

**Advanced tip:** Vary articulations to include the following:

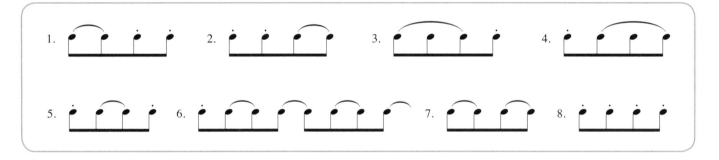

Day 1: A minor, E♭ minor

Day 2: D minor, G♯ minor

Day 3: G minor, C♯ minor

Day 4: C minor, F♯ minor

Day 5: F minor, B minor

Day 6: B♭ minor, E minor

Day 7: Repeat all

# FINGER MOBILITY

Strive for evenness of fingers. Repeat each measure four times, more if necessary. Increase speed with the metronome over time.

# ARTICULATION

Legato endurance study. Traditional French Carol, "Il est né, le divin Enfant." Use only the tip of the tongue; strive to keep the same articulation style and length throughout the exercise.
**Note:** Track 12 demonstrates measures 1–8.

# FLEXIBILITY

This exercise is a rhythmic variation of Week 1. Keep the smoothness of the interval while increasing the overall speed. Advanced players should work up to the same tempi in half notes.

## TONE

Continue to work on strengthening your tone from the bottom up. Work not only on matching tone quality throughout, but use increased air support and lip pressure to increase the volume. Slower is better.

**Advanced tip:** Strive to play at six distinct volume levels: *pp*, *p*, *mp*, *mf*, *f*, *ff*.

TRACK 14

## SCALES

Two-octave melodic minor scales. Focus on smooth, even fingers. Build in speed as appropriate. (See Track 2 for audio example.)

**Advanced tip:** Vary articulations to include the following:

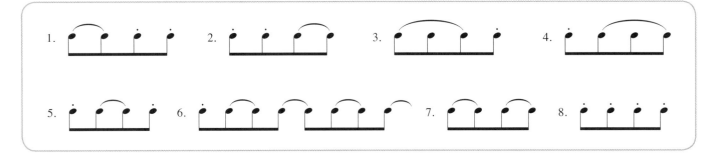

Day 1: A minor, E♭ minor

Day 2: D minor, G♯ minor

Day 3: G minor, C♯ minor

Day 4: C minor, F♯ minor

Day 5: F minor, B minor

Day 6: B♭ minor, E minor

Day 7: Repeat all

## FINGER MOBILITY

Strive for evenness of fingers. Repeat each measure four times, more if necessary. Increase speed with the metronome over time.

TRACK 15

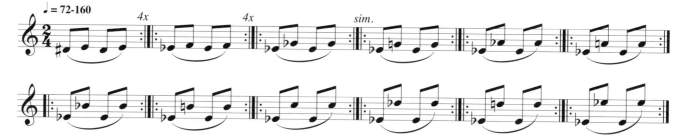

## ARTICULATION

Fast legato tongue. The goal is always to achieve beautiful tone with articulation, not articulation with tone inside. On this excerpt from J.S. Bach's *Partita in A Minor, BWV 1013* for flute alone, focus on the consistency of articulation while maintaining beauty of sound throughout. Practice this slurred to get a feel for the phrase shape, then add in the articulation gently, so that it merely "articulates" the phrase.

TRACK 16

## FLEXIBILITY

This exercise is a rhythmic variation of Week 2. Keep the smoothness of the interval while increasing the overall speed. Advanced players should work up to the same tempi in half notes.

TRACK 17

# WEEK 5

## TONE

Remember to consider vowel shape as you ascend. Does your vowel shape stay the same or change? It's different for everyone, so find what works for you. Mark it in your music, so you can be consistent in your practice. Slower is better.

TRACK 18

## SCALES

Expanding scales. Starting with the first two tones of the major scale, repeat four times. Then add in the third note; repeat four times. Continue through the pattern until you've expanded to a full two octaves.

**Note:** Track 19 demonstrates up to one octave.

**Advanced tip:** In addition to all slurred, play all tongued.

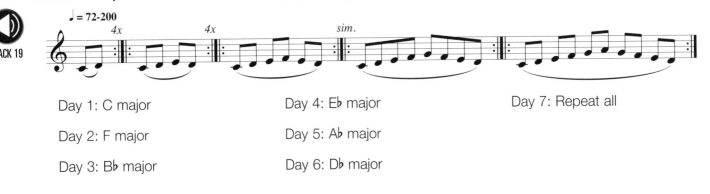

TRACK 19

Day 1: C major

Day 2: F major

Day 3: B♭ major

Day 4: E♭ major

Day 5: A♭ major

Day 6: D♭ major

Day 7: Repeat all

## FINGER MOBILITY

Strive for evenness of fingers. Repeat each measure four times, more if necessary. Increase speed with the metronome over time.

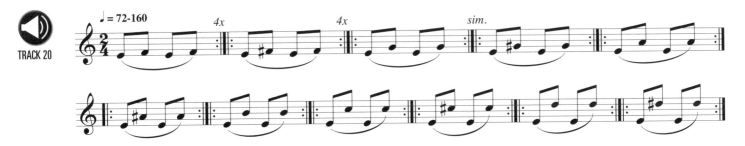

TRACK 20

## ARTICULATION

Staccato single-tongue study. Play each note with a bouncy, short release. Match releases through the exercise. Remember to use your support.

**TRACK 21**

## FLEXIBILITY

Continue to work on flexibility through the octaves. While some lip and jaw movement is necessary, be sensitive and keep the motion to a minimum to facilitate smooth leaps. Advanced players should work up to the same tempi in half notes.

**TRACK 22**

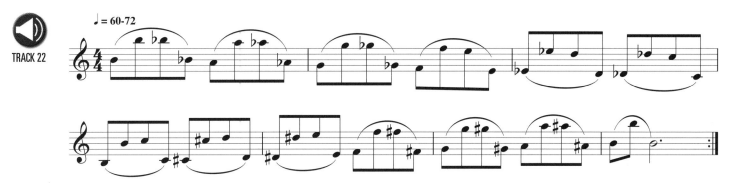

# WEEK 6

## TONE

Expanding upward into the middle register. Be aware of the vowel shape changes that occur as you ascend, and continue to build strength on the bottom. Slower is better.

TRACK 23

## SCALES

Expanding scales. Starting with the first two tones of the major scale, repeat four times. Then add in the third note; repeat four times. Continue through the pattern until you've expanded to a full two octaves. (See Track 19 for audio example.)

**Advanced tip:** In addition to all slurred, play all tongued.

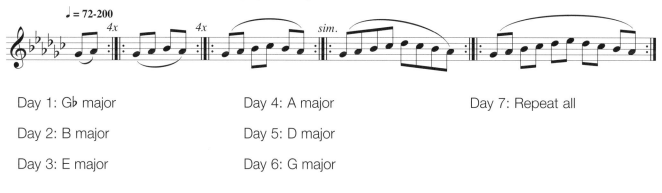

| Day 1: G♭ major | Day 4: A major | Day 7: Repeat all |
|---|---|---|
| Day 2: B major | Day 5: D major | |
| Day 3: E major | Day 6: G major | |

## FINGER MOBILITY

Strive for evenness of fingers. Repeat each measure four times, more if necessary. Increase speed with the metronome over time.

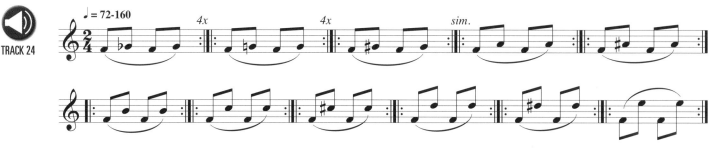

TRACK 24

# ARTICULATION

Staccato single-tongue study. Play each note with a bouncy, short release. Match releases through the exercise. Remember to use your support.

**TRACK 25**

# FLEXIBILITY

Velocity Study. Increase speed over time, paying particular attention to how both lip and jaw movement work together to facilitate the octave changes. When in doubt, aim the air down.

**TRACK 26**

## TONE

Middle C♯. Often cited as the worst note on the flute, middle C♯ has a nasty reputation for being wildly sharp. Part of the problem lies in the construction of the flute, but it can be overcome with a change in perception. Play the following exercise without changing the embouchure. Slower is better.

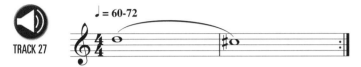

**TRACK 27**

Notice how high the C♯ wants to sound? Now play the following exercise without changing the embouchure.

**TRACK 28**

Do you hear how much lower the C♯ sounds? If we think of the middle C♯ as a *low* register note, by attaching it to the lower register it has much more resonance and is much better in tune. Spend some time with the following exercise to work on attaching C♯ to the low register.

**TRACK 29**

## SCALES

Expanding scales. Starting with the first two tones of the natural minor scale, repeat four times. Then add in the third note, repeat four times. Continue through the pattern until you've expanded to a full two octaves. (See Track 19 for audio example.)

**Advanced tip:** In addition to all slurred, play all tongued.

Day 1: A minor

Day 2: D minor

Day 3: G minor

Day 4: C minor

Day 5: F minor

Day 6: B♭ minor

Day 7: Repeat all

# FINGER MOBILITY

Strive for evenness of fingers. Repeat each measure four times, more if necessary. Increase speed with the metronome over time.

TRACK 30

# ARTICULATION

Staccato single-tongue study. Play each note with a bouncy, short release. Match releases through the exercise. Remember to use your support.

TRACK 31

# FLEXIBILITY

With the focus on the primary note, strive to maintain consistency of sound on the upper note while blowing through the intervals to create a seamless line.

**Note:** Track 32 demonstrates only the original.

TRACK 32

# WEEK 8

## TONE

Continuing the C# study from Week 7. Play the exercise with the new idea of extending your concept of *low* register to middle C#. Try it with a tuner and notice the difference. Slower is better.

**TRACK 33**

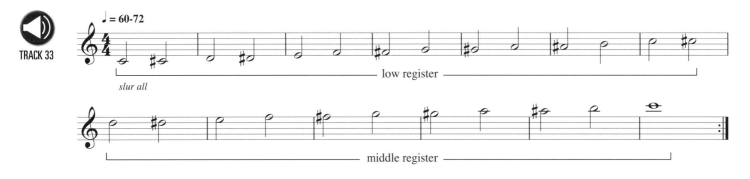

## SCALES

Expanding scales. Starting with the first two tones of the natural minor scale, repeat four times. Then add in the third note; repeat four times. Continue through the pattern until you've expanded to a full two octaves. (See Track 19 for audio example.)

**Advanced tip:** In addition to all slurred, play all tongued.

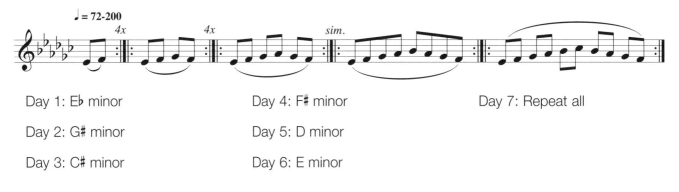

Day 1: E♭ minor          Day 4: F# minor          Day 7: Repeat all

Day 2: G# minor          Day 5: D minor

Day 3: C# minor          Day 6: E minor

## FINGER MOBILITY

Strive for evenness of fingers. Repeat each measure four times, more if necessary. Increase speed with the metronome over time.

**TRACK 34**

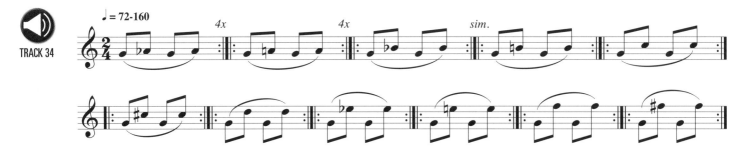

## ARTICULATION

Continue the use of the single tongue. Work up to a speed of ♩ = 112.

**TRACK 35**

(all single tongue)

Continue as in Week 5.

## FLEXIBILITY

Using the exercise from Week 7, play with the following variation:

**TRACK 36**

# WEEK 9

## TONE

Continue to listen for the quality and intonation of your middle C♯. These notes on the flute are what I call the Danger Zone. Each one has its own pitch tendencies and colors. Strive to make them as homogeneous as possible. Slower is better.

**Advanced tip:** Play this exercise both with and without vibrato, noting any differences in pitch.

TRACK 37

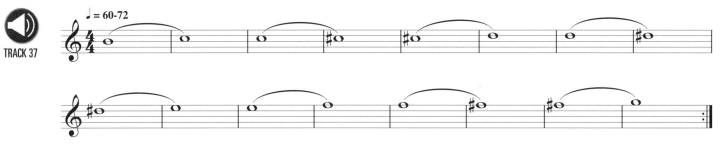

## SCALES

Expanding scales. Starting with the first two tones of the harmonic minor scale, repeat four times. Then add in the third note; repeat four times. Continue through the pattern until you've expanded to a full two octaves. (See Track 19 for audio example.)

**Advanced tip:** In addition to all slurred, play all tongued.

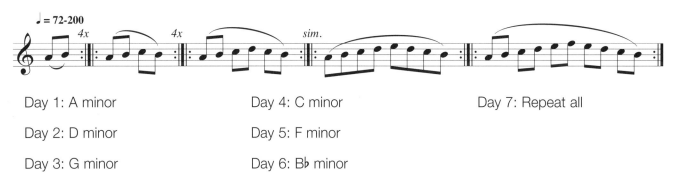

Day 1: A minor

Day 2: D minor

Day 3: G minor

Day 4: C minor

Day 5: F minor

Day 6: B♭ minor

Day 7: Repeat all

## FINGER MOBILITY

Strive for evenness of fingers. Repeat each measure four times, more if necessary. Increase speed with the metronome over time.

TRACK 38

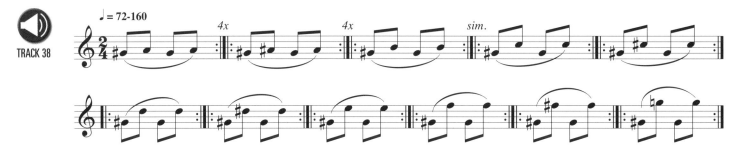

## ARTICULATION

Continue the use of the single tongue. Work up to a speed of ♩= 96.

**TRACK 39**

Continue as in Week 5.

## FLEXIBILITY

Using the exercise from Week 7, play with the following variation:

**TRACK 40**

# WEEK 10

## TONE

Danger Zone study. Continue to listen for consistency of quality and intonation as you play your way through. Remember to listen to the C#s, envisioning them as low-register notes. Slower is better.

**Advanced tip:** Play with and without vibrato, noticing any differences in intonation.

**TRACK 41**

## SCALES

Expanding scales. Starting with the first two tones of the harmonic minor scale, repeat four times. Then add in the third note; repeat four times. Continue through the pattern until you've expanded to a full two octaves. (See Track 19 for audio example.)

**Advanced tip:** In addition to all slurred, play all tongued.

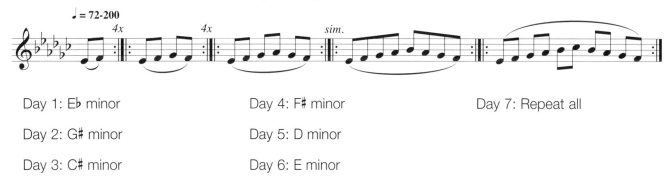

Day 1: E♭ minor        Day 4: F♯ minor        Day 7: Repeat all

Day 2: G♯ minor        Day 5: D minor

Day 3: C♯ minor        Day 6: E minor

## FINGER MOBILITY

Strive for evenness of fingers. Repeat each measure four times, more if necessary. Increase speed with the metronome over time.

**TRACK 42**

## ARTICULATION

Joachim Andersen, *Etude in A Minor, Op. 33, No. 2*. Play with a single tongue throughout. Strive to begin and end the etude with the same articulation style and length.

**Note:** The audio track demonstrates measures 1–16.

## FLEXIBILITY

Using the exercise from Week 7, play with the following variation:

Repeat with beginning notes:

## TONE

By now you should be more comfortable working in the Danger Zone. Here's an exercise that approaches it from above. Slower is better.

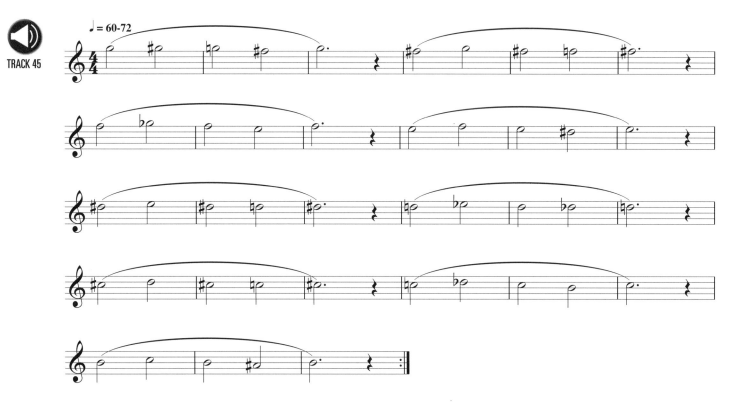

## SCALES

Expanding scales. Starting with the first two tones of the melodic minor scale, repeat four times. Then add in the third note; repeat four times. Continue through the pattern until you've expanded to a full two octaves. (See Track 19 for audio example.)

**Advanced tip:** In addition to all slurred, play all tongued.

Day 1: A minor

Day 2: D minor

Day 3: G minor

Day 4: C minor

Day 5: F minor

Day 6: B♭ minor

Day 7: Repeat all

# FINGER MOBILITY

Strive for evenness of fingers. Repeat each measure four times, more if necessary. Increase speed with the metronome over time. Also, play this exercise up one octave.

TRACK 46

# ARTICULATION

Double tongue. This exercise is designed to separate the front and back articulations to focus on evenness of execution. "T" and "K" are often used when discussing double tongue syllables, but the "D" and "G" are preferable because they are softer syllables, resulting in less tongue sound. Play each measure four times as noted.

TRACK 47

# FLEXIBILITY

Using the exercise from Week 7, play with the following variation:

TRACK 48

# WEEK 12

## TONE

Bottom-register flexibility. Play these expanding intervals very slowly, while trying to fill the intervals with sound. Keep a healthy *mezzo forte* to *forte* dynamic throughout, and concentrate on keeping the throat open through the note changes. Slower is better.

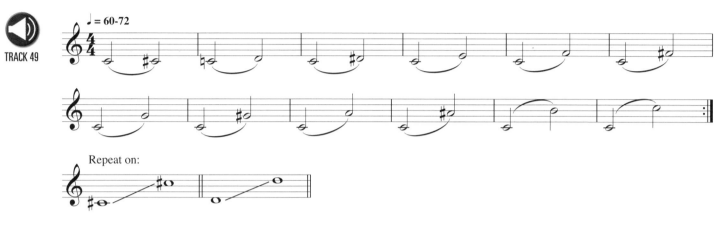

TRACK 49

## SCALES

Expanding scales. Starting with the first two tones of the melodic minor scale, repeat four times. Then add in the third note; repeat four times. Continue through the pattern until you've expanded to a full two octaves. (See Track 19 for audio example.)

**Advanced tip:** In addition to all slurred, play all tongued.

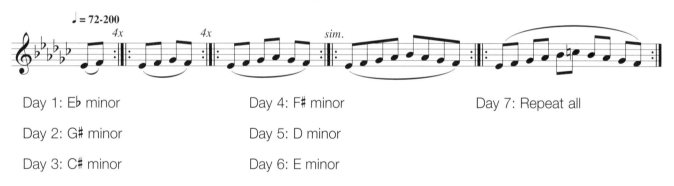

Day 1: E♭ minor      Day 4: F♯ minor      Day 7: Repeat all

Day 2: G♯ minor      Day 5: D minor

Day 3: C♯ minor      Day 6: E minor

## FINGER MOBILITY

Strive for evenness of fingers. Repeat each measure four times, more if necessary. Increase speed with the metronome over time. Also, play this exercise up one octave.

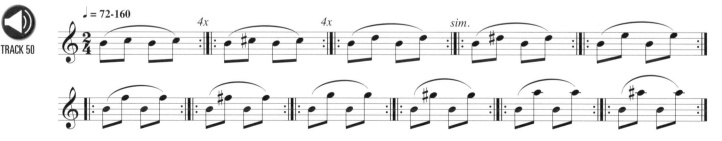

TRACK 50

## ARTICULATION

Double tongue. Play the following on any or all of your major and minor scales.

**TRACK 51**

Continue eight articulations
per note on a two-octave scale.

## FLEXIBILITY

Using the exercise from Week 7, play with the following variation.
**Note:** Track 52 demonstrates only the original.

**TRACK 52**

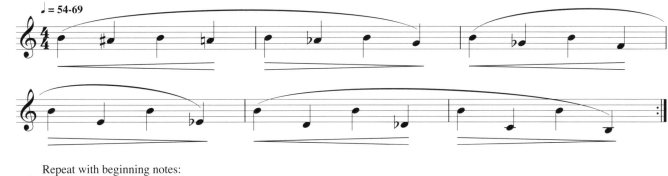

Repeat with beginning notes:

## TONE

Bottom-register flexibility. Play these expanding intervals very slowly, while trying to fill the intervals with sound. Be aware of keeping the throat open, and note which vowel sounds work best for you. Slower is better.

**TRACK 53**

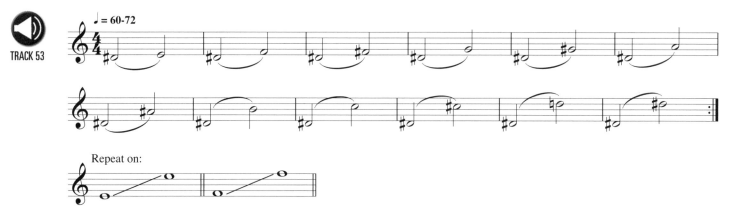

## SCALES

Ascending triplets. Focus on keeping the fingers close to the keys and the triplets even. Increase speed as possible.

**Advanced tip:** Vary articulations to include the following:

**TRACK 54**

C major, A♭ major, E major

## FINGER MOBILITY

Strive for evenness of fingers. Repeat each measure four times, more if necessary. Increase speed with the metronome over time. Also, play this exercise up one octave.

**TRACK 55**

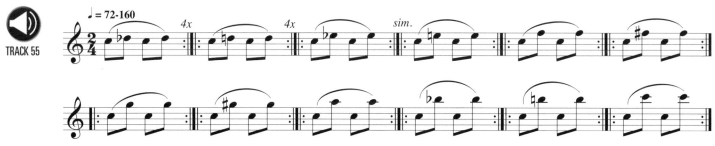

## ARTICULATION

Double tongue. Play the following on all your major and minor scales.

TRACK 56

Continue four articulations
per note on a two-octave scale.

## FLEXIBILITY

Using the exercise from Week 7, play with the following variation.
**Note:** Track 57 demonstrates only the original.

TRACK 57

Repeat with beginning notes:

# WEEK 14

## TONE

Bottom-register flexibility. Play these expanding intervals very slowly, while trying to fill the intervals with sound. Repeat up one half and one whole step. Slower is better.

**TRACK 58**

## SCALES

Ascending triplets. Focus on keeping the fingers close to the keys and the triplets even. Increase speed as possible. (See Track 54 for audio example.)

**Advanced tip:** Vary articulations to include the following:

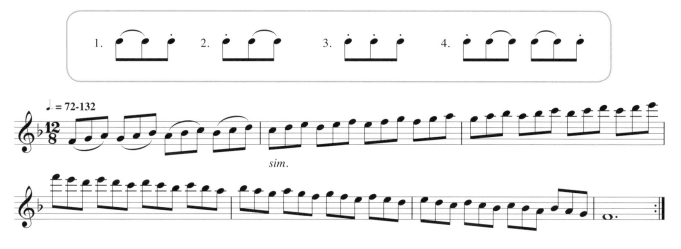

F major, D♭ major, A major

## FINGER MOBILITY

Strive for evenness of fingers. Repeat each measure four times, more if necessary. Increase speed with the metronome over time. Also, play this exercise up one octave.

**TRACK 59**

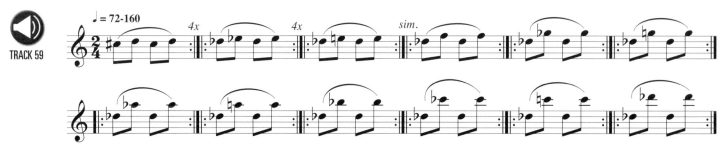

## ARTICULATION

Double tongue. Play the following on all your major and minor scales.

**TRACK 60**

Continue two articulations
per note on a two-octave scale.

## FLEXIBILITY

Play as smoothly as possible, transposing up both one half and one whole step. Advanced players should work up to the same tempi for the half note.

**TRACK 61**

# WEEK 15

## TONE

Slow whole-tone and chromatic scales. Listen carefully to the distance between the whole and half steps. Train your ear to begin to hear and anticipate the distance between the different intervals. Playing in tune doesn't rely on your fingers, but in where you place each note. Slower is better.

**Advanced tip:** Play this with a tuner, training your ear to hear the interval before playing.

**TRACK 62**

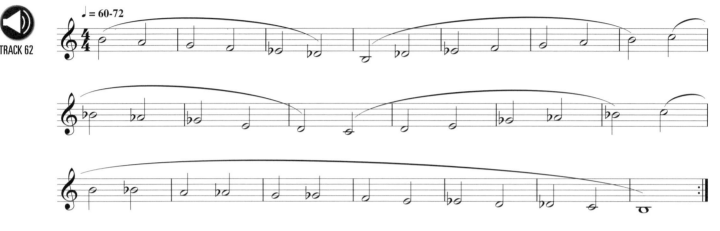

## SCALES

Ascending triplets. Focus on keeping the fingers close to the keys and the triplets even. Increase speed as possible. (See Track 54 for audio example.)

**Advanced tip:** Vary articulations to include the following:

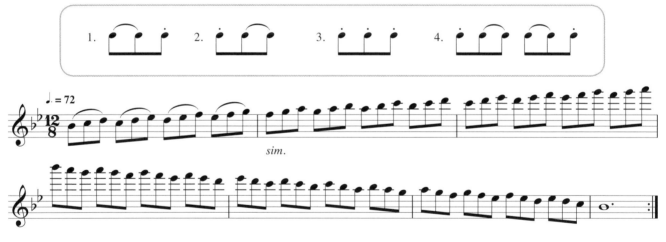

Bb major, Gb major, D major

## FINGER MOBILITY

Strive for evenness of fingers. Repeat each measure four times, more if necessary. Increase speed with the metronome over time. Also, play this exercise up one octave.

**TRACK 63**

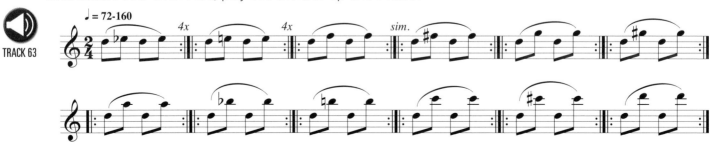

## ARTICULATION

The "running" double tongue, using one alternating articulation per note. Play on all major and minor scales.

## FLEXIBILITY

For velocity. Also, transpose up a half step and a whole step. Advanced players should work up to the same tempi in half notes.

# WEEK 16

## TONE

Expanding low-register intervals. Play as smoothly as possible. Slower is better.
**Advanced tip:** Play at different dynamic levels, with crescendo and diminuendo throughout.

**TRACK 66**

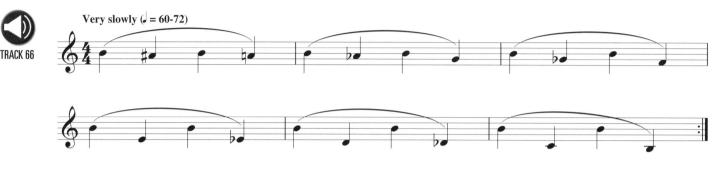

## SCALES

Ascending triplets. Focus on keeping the fingers close to the keys and the triplets even. Increase speed as possible. (See Track 54 for audio example.)
**Advanced tip:** Vary articulations to include the following:

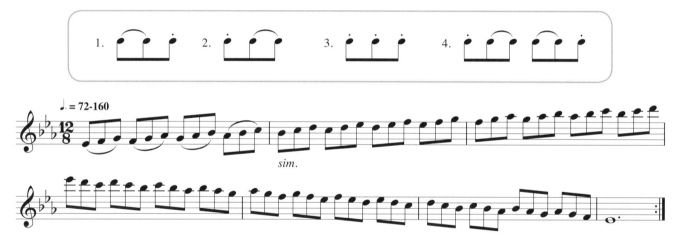

Eb major, B major, G major

## FINGER MOBILITY

Strive for evenness of fingers. Repeat each measure four times, more if necessary. Increase speed with the metronome over time. Also, play this exercise up one octave.

**TRACK 67**

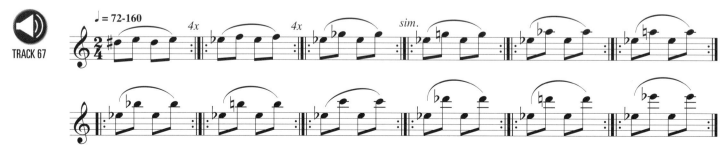

## ARTICULATION

Double-tongue study. Play this pattern on all major and minor scales.

TRACK 68

## FLEXIBILITY

For velocity. Keep intervals smooth and even by keeping the throat open and by using fluid motion with the lips and jaw.

**Advanced tip:** Use a tuner to check the octaves. Work up to same tempi as half notes.

TRACK 69

## TONE

Variation on Week 16. Use the following rhythm and dynamic changes throughout. Slower is better.

**TRACK 70**

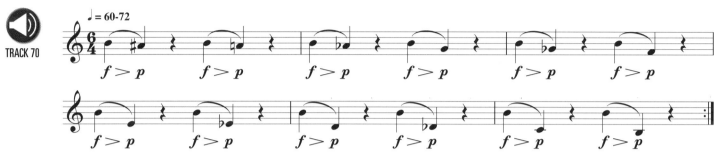

## SCALES

Wandering triplets. Focus on keeping the fingers close to the keys and the triplets even. Increase speed as possible.

**Advanced tip:** Vary articulations to include the following:

**TRACK 71**

C major, D♭ major

# FINGER MOBILITY

Strive for evenness of fingers. Repeat each measure four times, more if necessary. Increase speed with the metronome over time. Also, play this exercise up one octave.

**TRACK 72**

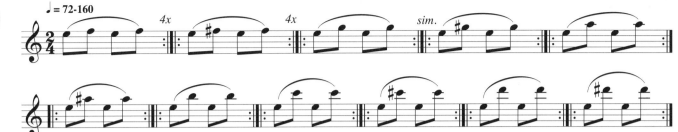

# ARTICULATION

Double-tongue pattern. Repeat on all major and minor scales.

**TRACK 73**

Continue on a two-octave scale.

# FLEXIBILITY

Continued velocity. Also, play transposed up a half step and a whole step.

**TRACK 74**

Continue to:

# WEEK 18

## TONE

Variation on Week 16. Use the following rhythm and dynamic changes throughout. Slower is better.

**TRACK 75**

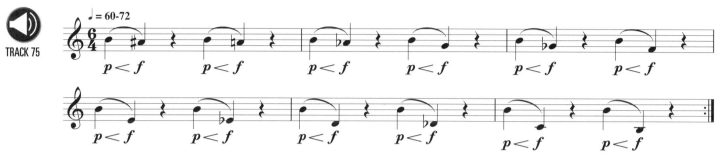

## SCALES

Wandering triplets. Focus on keeping the fingers close to the keys and the triplets even. Increase speed as possible. (See Track 71 for audio example.)

**Advanced tip:** Vary articulations to include the following:

D major, Eb major

# FINGER MOBILITY

Strive for evenness of fingers. Repeat each measure four times, more if necessary. Increase speed with the metronome over time. Also, play this exercise up one octave.

# ARTICULATION

Double-tongue pattern. Repeat on all major and minor scales.

Continue the pattern on a two-octave scale.

# FLEXIBILITY

Arpeggio study. A word on evenness of fingers and sound before velocity: Use the strength of your sound in the bottom register to propel you upward through the register. Rather than dipping "down" from the top, use your bottom sound to give you strength. It's similar to bending your knees before you jump; pretty hard to jump from straight and inflexible knees!

# WEEK 19

## TONE

Variation on Week 16. Use the following rhythm and dynamic changes throughout. Slower is better.

## SCALES

Wandering triplets. Focus on keeping the fingers close to the keys and the triplets even. Increase speed as possible. (See Track 71 for audio example.)

**Advanced tip:** Vary articulations to include the following:

E major, F major

# FINGER MOBILITY

Strive for evenness of fingers. Repeat each measure four times, more if necessary. Increase speed with the metronome over time. Also, play this exercise up one octave.

# ARTICULATION

Double-tongue study. Georges Bizet, "Les Toréadors" from *Carmen Suite No. 1*. Keep the articulation crisp and even.

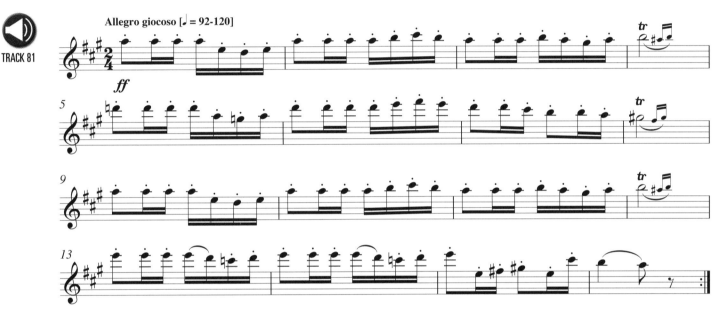

# FLEXIBILITY

Arpeggio study. Remember to let the strength of the bottom register propel you upward through the study.

## TONE

Variation on Week 16. Use the following rhythm and dynamic changes throughout. Slower is better.

TRACK 83

## SCALES

Wandering triplets. Focus on keeping the fingers close to the keys and the triplets even. Increase speed as possible. (See Track 71 for audio example.)

**Advanced tip:** Vary articulations to include the following:

Gb major, G major

## FINGER MOBILITY

Strive for evenness of fingers. Repeat each measure four times, more if necessary. Increase speed with the metronome over time.

TRACK 84

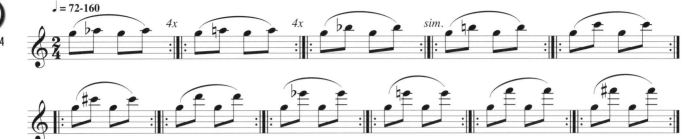

## ARTICULATION

Joachim Andersen, *Etude in A Minor, Op. 33, No. 2*. (See Week 10, page 22.) Play twice through, using the articulation patterns noted below:

Double tongue the *first note* of each measure. The audio track demonstrates measures 1–16.

TRACK 85

Double tongue the *first two notes* of each measure. The audio track demonstrates measures 1–16.

TRACK 86

## FLEXIBILITY

Continued velocity. Keep the throat open and be aware of changing vowel shapes.

TRACK 87

# WEEK 21

## TONE

Low-register dynamic flexibility. Slower is better.
**Advanced tip:** Practice this with a tuner through the crescendo and diminuendo.

**TRACK 88**

## SCALES

Scale pattern with thirds. Keep the hands relaxed and close to the keys. If you feel finger tension, try relaxing your wrists. Release the tension through the palm, the base of the hand and the wrist. Increase speed as possible.
**Advanced tip:** Vary articulations to include the following:

Ab major, A major

## FINGER MOBILITY

Strive for evenness of fingers. Repeat each measure four times, more if necessary. Increase speed with the metronome over time.

TRACK 89

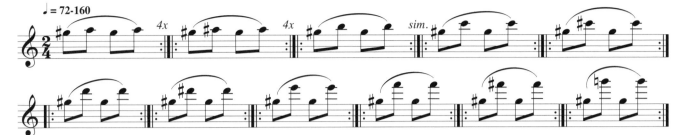

## ARTICULATION

Joachim Andersen, *Etude in A Minor, Op. 33, No. 2*. (See Week 10, page 22.) Play twice through, using the articulation patterns noted below:

Double tongue the *first three notes* of each measure.

TRACK 90

Double tongue the *first four notes* of each measure.

TRACK 91

## FLEXIBILITY

Arpeggio study. Work toward good intonation on the Danger Zone notes.

TRACK 92

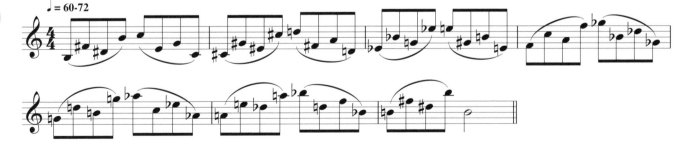

## TONE

Claude Debussy, *Prelude to the Afternoon of a Faun*. This excerpt is all about color and dynamic, highlighting all the techniques you have been working on. Watch the middle C#, being careful to give it color and correct intonation. Listen for all the whole steps and half steps in the first two measures, and smooth out the larger intervals in measures 3 and 4. Your goal is precision of sound, not an accurate orchestral performance tempo.

**TRACK 93**

## SCALES

Scale pattern with thirds. Keep the hands relaxed and close to the keys. If you feel finger tension, try relaxing your wrists. Release the tension through the palm, the base of the hand and the wrist. Increase speed as possible.

**Advanced tip:** Vary articulations to include the following:

B♭ major, B major

# FINGER MOBILITY

Strive for evenness of fingers. Repeat each measure four times, more if necessary. Increase speed with the metronome over time.

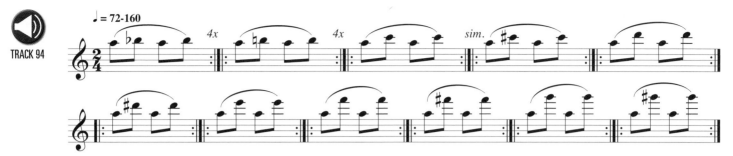

## ARTICULATION

Joachim Andersen, *Etude in A Minor, Op. 33, No. 2*. (See Week 10, page 22.) Play twice through, using the articulation patterns noted below:

Double tongue the *first five notes* of each measure.

Double tongue the *all notes* of each measure.

## FLEXIBILITY

Harmonics and intonation. Play the octave first as a harmonic, then switch to regular fingering. Transpose up one half step for one full octave.
**Note:** The audio track demonstrates C, C♯, and D.

# WEEK 23

## TONE

Expanding interval study. Play every two measures as a crescendo leading to the half note. Slower is better.

**TRACK 98**

## SCALES

Scale pattern with thirds. Keep the hands relaxed and close to the keys. If you feel finger tension, try relaxing your wrists. Release the tension through the palm, the base of the hand and the wrist. Increase speed as possible.

**Advanced tip:** Vary articulations to include the following:

**TRACK 99**

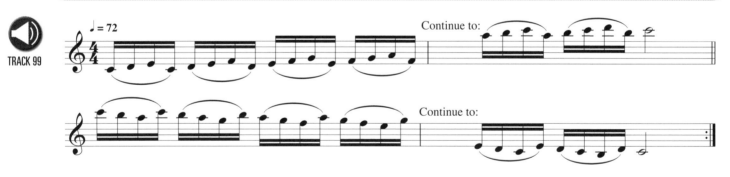

C major, A♭ major, E major, B♭ major, G♭ major, D major

## FINGER MOBILITY

Strive for evenness of fingers. Repeat each measure four times, more if necessary. Increase speed with the metronome over time.

**TRACK 100**

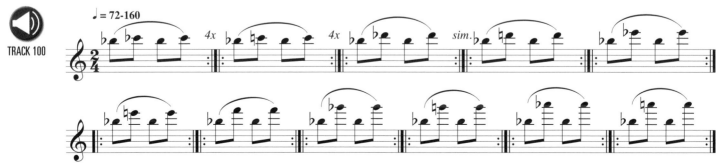

# ARTICULATION

J.S. Bach, *Flute Sonata in C Major, BWV 1033*, movement 2. This is a test of articulation accuracy and endurance. To begin, first practice completely slurred to get the finger changes accurate and smooth. Work up to slurring in shorter groups of four and two. Finally, start double tonguing slowly and evenly; gradually work up the tempo. You have two weeks for this study.

**Note:** The audio track demonstrates measures 1–20.

TRACK 101

# FLEXIBILITY

Harmonics study. Work on careful placement of the first two harmonics in the series, listening carefully for intonation. Transpose up one half step for one full octave.

TRACK 102

## TONE

The middle register. Here, we're matching tone through the Danger Zone into the low register. Slower is better.

**TRACK 103**

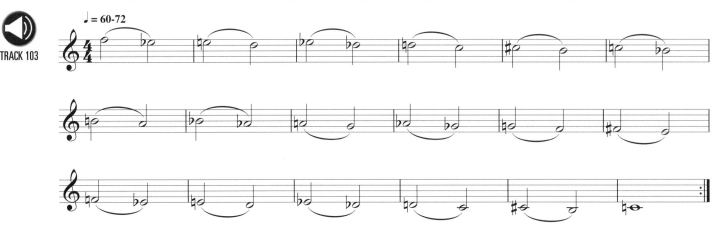

## SCALES

Scale pattern with thirds. Keep the hands relaxed and close to the keys. If you feel finger tension, try relaxing your wrists. Release the tension through the palm, the base of the hand, and the wrist. Increase speed as possible.

**Advanced tip:** Vary articulations to include the following:

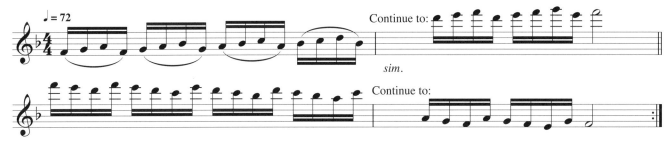

F major, D♭ major, A major, E♭ major, B major, G major

## FINGER MOBILITY

Strive for evenness of fingers. Repeat each measure four times, more if necessary. Increase speed with the metronome over time.

**TRACK 104**

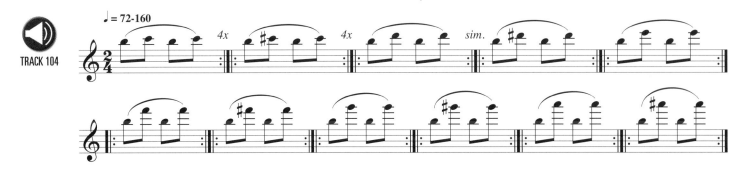

## ARTICULATION

J.S. Bach, *Flute Sonata in C Major, BWV 1033*, movement 2. See the practice instructions for Week 23, page 49.

## FLEXIBILITY

Harmonics study. Work on careful placement of the first two harmonics in the series, listening carefully for intonation. Transpose up one half step for one full octave.

**Note:** Track 105 demonstrates only the original.

## TONE

Camille Saint-Saëns, "The Aquarium" from *Carnival of the Animals*. Focus on making the difference between the middle and low registers as smooth as possible. Slower is better.

**Note:** Track 106 demonstrates measures 1–8.

**TRACK 106**

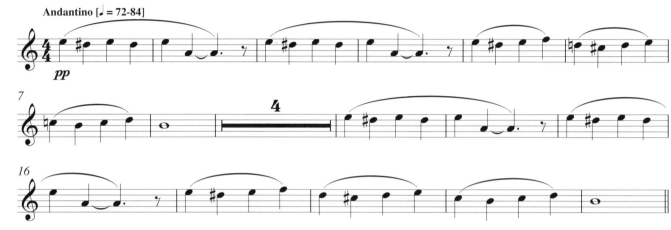

## SCALES

Scales with neighbors. Keep it even, and don't rush the neighbor. Increase speed as possible.

**Advanced tip:** Vary articulations to include the following:

**TRACK 107**

C major, A♭ major, E major

## FINGER MOBILITY

Strive for evenness of fingers. Repeat each measure four times, more if necessary. Increase speed with the metronome over time.

**TRACK 108**

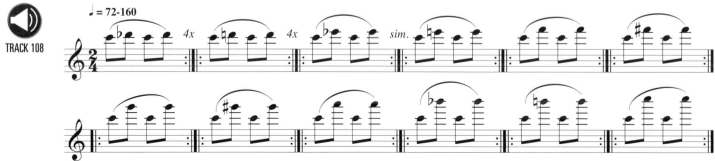

## ARTICULATION

Double tonguing with expanding intervals. Be sure to carefully coordinate tongue and finger movement.
Practice the pattern on all major scales.

TRACK 109

## FLEXIBILITY

Octave study. Make the intervals as smooth as possible, gradually adding in velocity.

TRACK 110

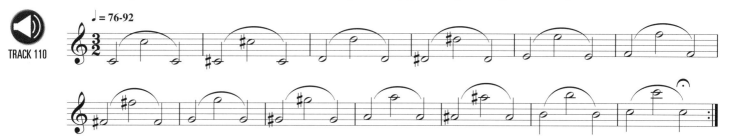

## TONE

The middle register. Feel as though the third note propels you into the half note. It's like bending your knees before you jump. Use the crescendo to help. Slower is better.

**TRACK 111**

## SCALES

Scales with neighbors. Keep it even, and don't rush the neighbor. Increase speed as possible. (See Track 107 for audio example.)

**Advanced tip:** Vary articulations to include the following:

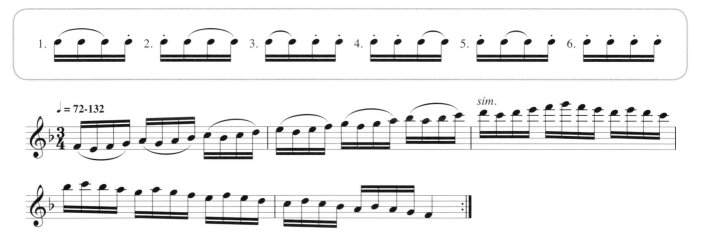

F major, D♭ major, A major

## FINGER MOBILITY

Strive for evenness of fingers. Repeat each measure four times, more if necessary. Increase speed with the metronome over time. Transpose on the indicated starting pitches.

**TRACK 112**

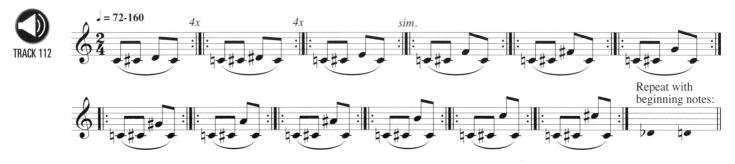

Repeat with
beginning notes:

## ARTICULATION

Camille Saint-Saëns, "Voliere" (no. 10) from *Carnival of the Animals*. This Voliere Study No. 1 will help solidify finger/tongue coordination. The notation is different from the original; this acts as a preparatory study to the orchestral part. Start at ♩ = 72 and work up to ♩ = 144.

**Note:** The audio track demonstrates measures 1–2.

**TRACK 113**

## FLEXIBILITY

Chromatic octave study. As always, emphasis should be on the bottom notes. Increase tempo as possible.

**TRACK 114**

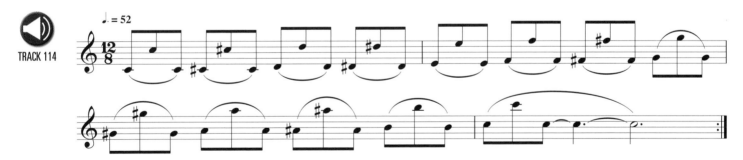

## TONE

Octave study. Crescendo into the octave jump to smooth out any bumps.

**TRACK 115**

## SCALES

Scales with neighbors. Keep it even, and don't rush the neighbor. Increase speed as possible. (See Track 107 for audio example.)

**Advanced tip:** Vary articulations to include the following:

D major, B♭ major, G♭ major

## FINGER MOBILITY

Strive for evenness of fingers. Repeat each measure four times, more if necessary. Increase speed with the metronome over time. Transpose on the indicated starting pitches.

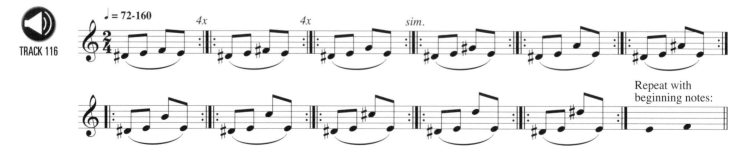

**TRACK 116**

Repeat with
beginning notes:

## ARTICULATION

Camille Saint-Saëns, "Voliere" (no. 10) from *Carnival of the Animals*. This Voliere Study No. 2 helps your tongue build up endurance required for this excerpt. While the notation duplicated here is as it exists in the orchestral score, this study requires that you double tongue each note, twice the effort required for the final version. If your tongue starts to feel fatigued, make sure your jaw and throat are free of tension, and that your head isn't leaning forward.

**Note:** The audio track demonstrates measures 1–2.

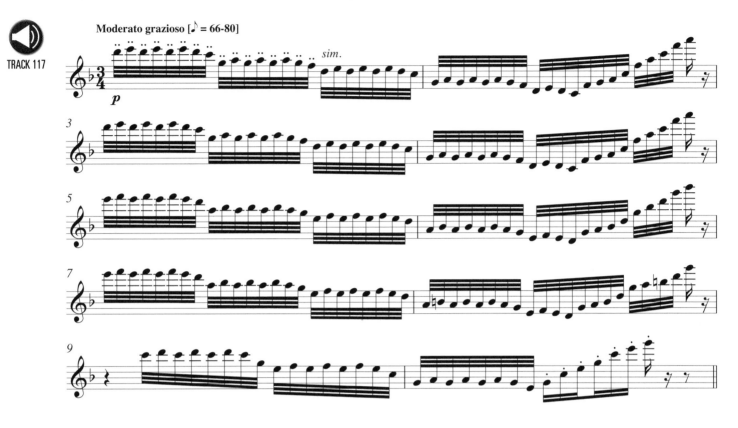

## FLEXIBILITY

Quick octave study. Always be thinking ahead for the octave changes. Anticipate the lip, jaw, and air movement required for successful execution of the octaves. Increase the tempo as possible.

## TONE

Middle-register study. Continue to experiment with vowel shapes to find the best position for you. Slower is better.

**Advanced tip:** Play these with a variety of colors and dynamics, using the tuner for added support.

## SCALES

Scales with lower neighbors. Keep it even, and don't rush the lower neighbor. Increase speed as possible. (See Track 107 for audio example.)

**Advanced tip:** Vary articulations to include the following:

E♭ major, B major, G major

## FINGER MOBILITY

Strive for evenness of fingers. Repeat each measure four times, more if necessary. Increase speed with the metronome over time. Transpose on the indicated starting pitches.

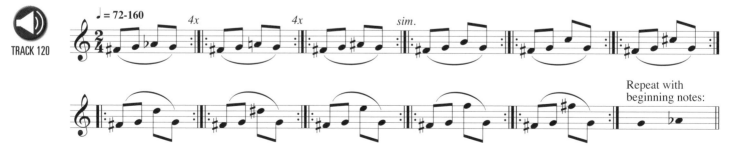

Repeat with beginning notes:

## ARTICULATION

Camille Saint-Saëns, "Voliere" (no. 10) from *Carnival of the Animals*. This Voliere Study No. 3 is duplicated as it exists in the orchestral score. If your tongue starts to feel fatigued, make sure your jaw and throat are free of tension, and that your head isn't leaning forward.

**Note:** The audio track demonstrates measures 1–2.

**TRACK 121**

## FLEXIBILITY

Octaves and fifths. Start slowly with an open, relaxed throat. Increase speed over time. (See Track 126 for audio example.)

**Note:** The audio track demonstrates C, C♯, and D.

**TRACK 122**

## TONE

Middle-register study. Play slowly with a tuner, training your ear to hear the distance of the half steps and whole steps. Slower is better.

**TRACK 123**

## SCALES

Fun with mixed meter! Play all your major and minor scales in the following pattern. Increase speed as possible.

**TRACK 124**

## FINGER MOBILITY

Strive for evenness of fingers. Repeat each measure four times, more if necessary. Increase speed with the metronome over time. Transpose on the indicated starting pitches.

**TRACK 125**

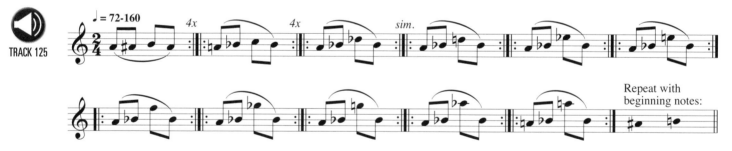

## ARTICULATION

Felix Mendelssohn, "Scherzo" from *A Midsummer Night's Dream*. Begin this study with the following articulations only. Your goal is accuracy of fingers and rhythm, lining up subdivisions and articulations precisely.

**Note:** The audio track demonstrates #2, measures 1–10 (beat 1).

**TRACK 126**

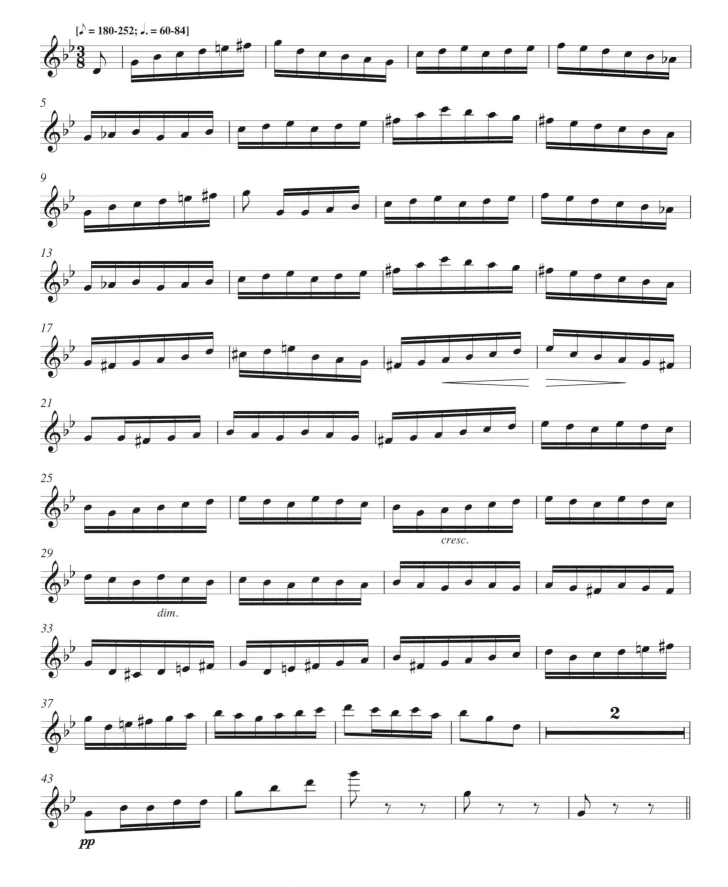

## FLEXIBILITY

This is one of the most difficult intervals to play on the flute. Work on hearing the interval in advance of playing it. You may find that you need to play both notes with standard fingerings first, then add in the harmonic fingering on the second note. Advanced players should try this exercise slurred.

TRACK 127

## TONE

Moving into the high register. Keep working to maintain quality of sound. If the quality doesn't match, stop and find a new vowel shape. Slower is better.

TRACK 128

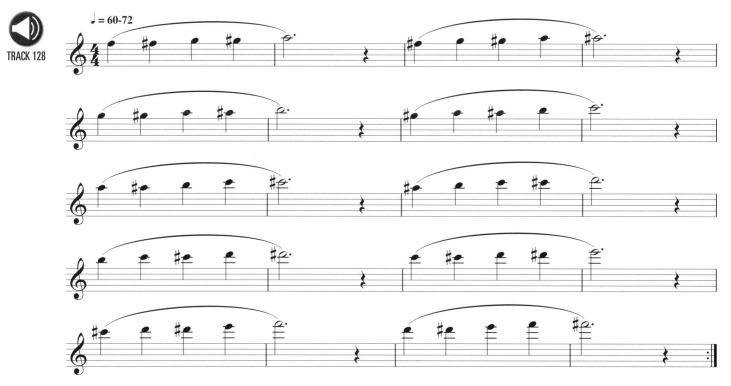

## SCALES

Fun with mixed meter! Play all your major and minor scales in the following pattern. Increase speed as possible.

TRACK 129

## FINGER MOBILITY

Strive for evenness of fingers. Repeat each measure four times, more if necessary. Increase speed with the metronome over time. Transpose on the indicated starting pitches.

TRACK 130

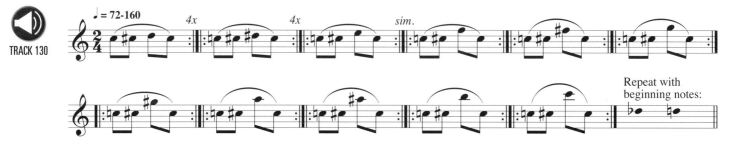

## ARTICULATION

Felix Mendelssohn, "Scherzo" from *A Midsummer Night's Dream*. Play this study, found on page 61, with the following articulations only. Your goal is accuracy of fingers and rhythm, lining up subdivisions and articulations precisely. Successful execution of the excerpt depends on the ability to hear the subdivisions and line up articulations accordingly.

**Note:** The audio track demonstrates #1, measures 1–10 (beat 1).

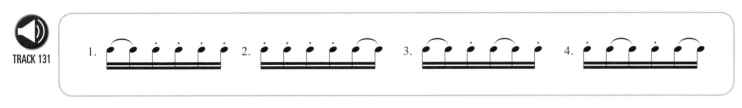

TRACK 131

## FLEXIBILITY

Expanding descending intervals. Transpose to starting pitches of D♭, D, E♭, E, and F.

TRACK 132

(all slurred)

# WEEK 31

## TONE

Richard Strauss, an excerpt from the opera *Salome*. This is a deceptively simple descending scale. Play the passage smooth and connected, but also with a captivating, projected sound.

**TRACK 133**

## SCALES

Inverted scales. Practice all slurred, all tongued, or with a variety of articulations. Increase speed as possible.

**TRACK 134**

C major, Ab major, E major

## FINGER MOBILITY

Strive for evenness of fingers. Repeat each measure four times, more if necessary. Increase speed with the metronome over time. Transpose on the indicated starting pitches.

**TRACK 135**

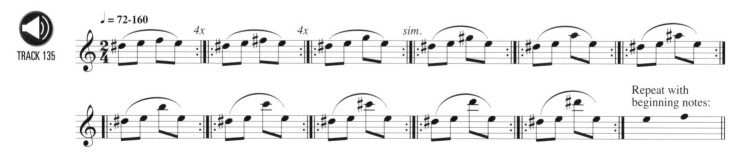

## ARTICULATION

Felix Mendelssohn, "Scherzo" from *A Midsummer Night's Dream*. (See page 61.) This week, we work on building the tongue accuracy and endurance to play this excerpt. The first variation requires a double-double tongue (each note double tongued). The second variation is a reverse double tongue (G-D-G-D-G-D), and the final version is as written with standard double tongue.

**Note:** The audio track demonstrates #1, measures 1–10 (downbeat).

TRACK 136

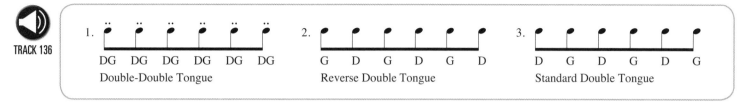

## FLEXIBILITY

Expanding descending intervals. Transpose to the beginning pitches of Gb, G, Ab, A, Bb, and B. (See Track 132 for audio example.)

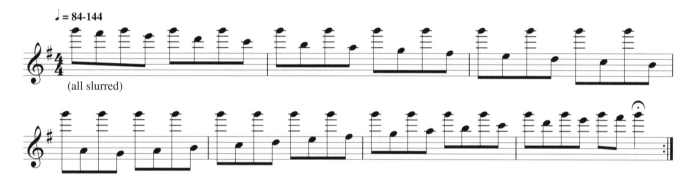

## TONE

Expanding into the high register. Slower is better.

**TRACK 137**

## SCALES

Inverted scales. Practice all slurred, all tongued, or with a variety of articulations. Increase speed as possible. (See Track 134 for audio example.)

F major, D♭ major, A major

## FINGER MOBILITY

Strive for evenness of fingers. Repeat each measure four times, more if necessary. Increase speed with the metronome over time. Transpose on the indicated starting pitches.

**TRACK 138**

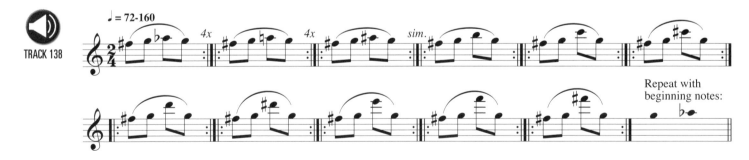

# ARTICULATION

Another use for the double tongue! Try playing your major and minor scales with this articulation pattern.

**TRACK 139**

D  G  D  D  G  D  D  G  D  D  G  D     D  G  D  D  G  D  D  G  D  D  G  D     D  G  D  D  G  D  D  G  D  D  G  D

D  G  D  D  G  D  D  G  D  D  G  D     D  G  D  D  G  D  D  G  D  D  G  D     D  G  D  D  G  D  D  G  D  D  G  D

D  G  D  D  G  D  D  G  D  D  G  D  D

# FLEXIBILITY

Ascending expanding intervals. Practice on C major, A♭ major, and E major.

**TRACK 140**

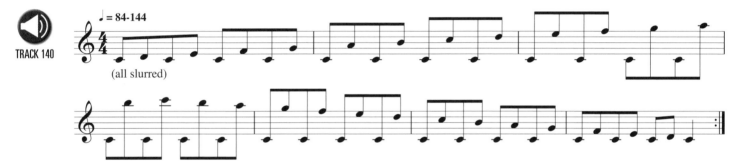

(all slurred)

## TONE

High-register study with diminuendo. Be careful not to go flat at the end of your diminuendo. Slower is better.

TRACK 141

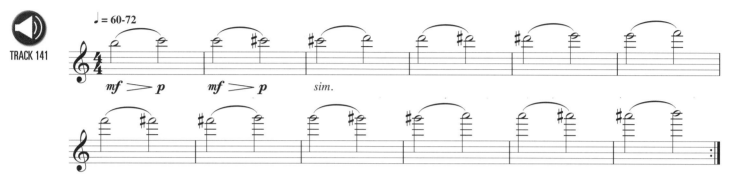

## SCALES

Inverted scales. Practice all slurred, all tongued, or with a variety of articulations. Increase speed as possible. (See Track 134 for audio example.)

B♭ major, G♭ major, D major

## FINGER MOBILITY

Strive for evenness of fingers. Repeat each measure four times, more if necessary. Increase speed with the metronome over time. Transpose on the indicated starting pitches.

TRACK 142

## ARTICULATION

Yet another use for the double tongue! Try playing your major and minor scales with this pattern.

D  G D  G D  G D  G  D  G D  G D  G D  G  D  G D  G D  G D  G  D  G D  G D  G D  G

D  G D  G D  G D  G  D  G D  G D  G D  G  D  G D  G D  G D  G  D  G D  G D

## FLEXIBILITY

Ascending expanding intervals. Practice on F major, D♭ major, and A major. (See Track 140 for audio example.)

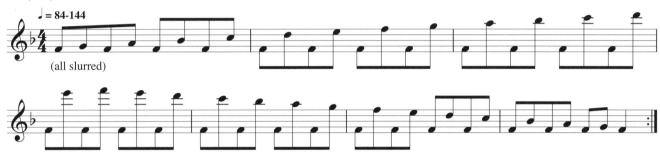

(all slurred)

## TONE

High-register soft dynamic. Exaggerate the diminuendo—get as soft as you can. Slower is better.
**Advanced tip:** Practice these with a tuner.

TRACK 144

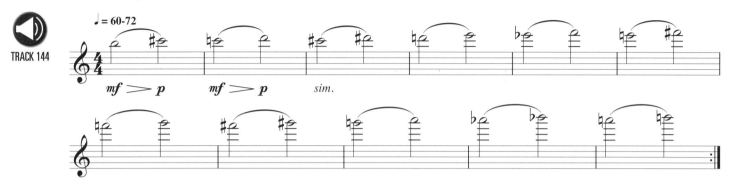

## SCALES

Inverted scales. Practice all slurred, all tongued, or with a variety of articulations. Increase speed as possible. (See Track 134 for audio example.)

E♭ major, B major, G major

## FINGER MOBILITY

Strive for evenness of fingers. Repeat each measure four times, more if necessary. Increase speed with the metronome over time. Transpose on the indicated starting pitches.

TRACK 145

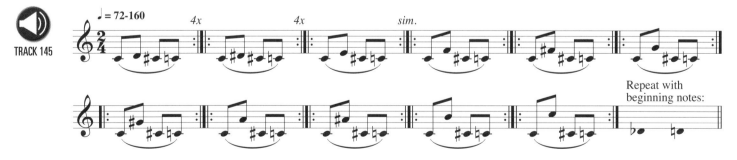

## ARTICULATION

Triple tonguing. Triple tonguing is the repetition of the pattern D-G-D. This preparatory exercise will help even out the pattern and increase flexibility. Play this pattern on all your one-octave major and minor scales.
**Note:** The audio track demonstrates F and G.

TRACK 146

| | | | | | | | |
|---|---|---|---|---|---|---|---|
| 1) | D | D | D | D | D | D | D |
| 2) | G | G | G | G | G | G | G |
| 3) | D | G | D | D | G | D | D |
| 4) | G | D | G | G | D | G | G |

## FLEXIBILITY

Ascending expanding intervals. Practice on B♭ major, G♭ major, and D major. (See Track 140 for audio example.)

(all slurred)

## TONE

High-register flexibility. These can be quite exhausting, so take your time. Exaggerate the dynamic contours. Slower is better.

**Advanced tip:** Play these with a tuner.

TRACK 147

## SCALES

Wandering scales; two octaves in a non-traditional format. Practice all slurred, all tongued, or with a variety of articulations. Increase speed as possible.

TRACK 148

C major, A♭ major, E major

## FINGER MOBILITY

Strive for evenness of fingers. Repeat each measure four times, more if necessary. Increase speed with the metronome over time. Transpose on the indicated starting pitches.

TRACK 149

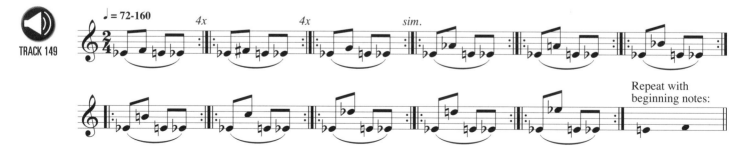

## ARTICULATION

Triple tongue. Play this one on all your one-octave major and minor scales, gradually increasing speed.

## FLEXIBILITY

Ascending expanding intervals. Practice on E♭ major, B major, and G major. (See Track 140 for audio example.)

# WEEK 36

## TONE

These can be quite exhausting, so take your time. Be sure to exaggerate the dynamic contours. Slower is better.

TRACK 151

## SCALES

Wandering scales; two octaves in a non-traditional format. Practice all slurred, all tongued, or with a variety of articulations. Increase speed as possible. (See Track 148 for audio example.)

F major, D♭ major, A major

## FINGER MOBILITY

Strive for evenness of fingers. Repeat each measure four times, more if necessary. Increase speed with the metronome over time. Transpose on the indicated starting pitches.

TRACK 152

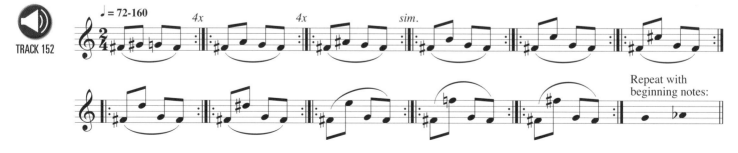

## ARTICULATION

Triple tongue. Play this one on all your one-octave major and minor scales, gradually increasing speed.

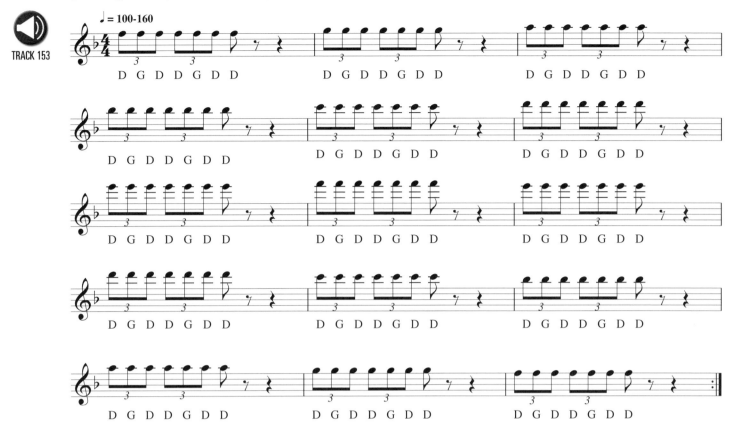

## FLEXIBILITY

High-register flexibility. Try to match the pitch and dynamic between the primary and harmonic notes.
**Note:** Track 154 demonstrates measures 1–6.

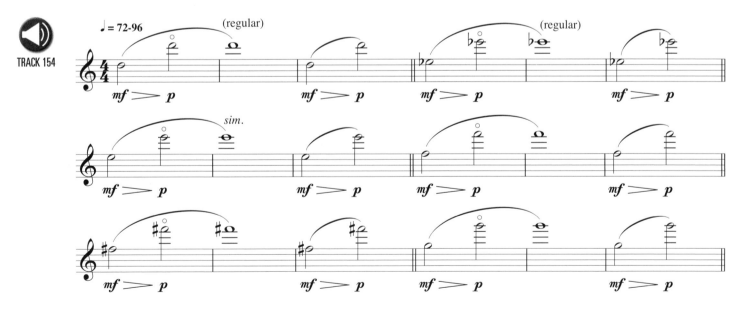

## TONE

Johannes Brahms, Symphony No. 4, movement 4. This excerpt requires flexibility throughout the high register. Focus not only on the beauty of sound from beginning to end, but also on maintaining a lovely phrase shape.

**TRACK 155**

## SCALES

Wandering scales; two octaves in a non-traditional format. Practice all slurred, all tongued, or with a variety of articulations. Increase speed as possible. (See Track 148 for audio example.)

Bb major, Gb major, D major

## FINGER MOBILITY

Strive for evenness of fingers. Repeat each measure four times, more if necessary. Increase speed with the metronome over time. Transpose on the indicated starting pitches.

**TRACK 156**

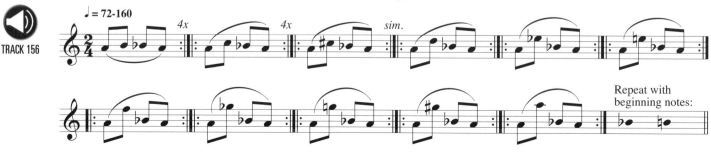

## ARTICULATION

Triple tongue. Play this on all your one-octave major and minor scales, gradually increasing speed.

D G D D G D D G D D G D    D G D D G D D G D D G D    D G D D G D D G D D G D

D G D D G D D G D D G D    D G D D G D D G D D G D    D G D D G D D G D D G D

D G D D G D D G D D G D    D G D D G D D

## FLEXIBILITY

Velocity in high-register octaves. Increase speed as possible.

## TONE

High-register octaves. Keep the throat open and relaxed, and the support constant. Slower is better.

## SCALES

Wandering scales; two octaves in a non-traditional format. Practice all slurred, all tongued, or with a variety of articulations. Increase speed as possible. (See Track 148 for audio example.)

Eb major, B major, G major

## FINGER MOBILITY

Strive for evenness of fingers. Repeat each measure four times, more if necessary. Increase speed with the metronome over time. Transpose on the indicated starting pitches.

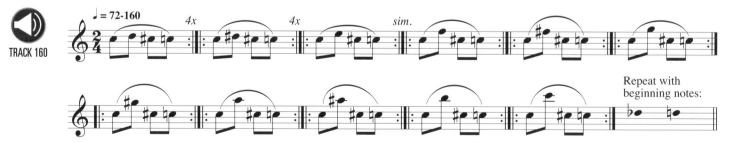

TRACK 160

# ARTICULATION

Non-continuous triple tongue. Play this on all your one-octave major and minor scales.

D    D D G D D    D D G D    D    D D G D D    D D G D    D    D D G D D    D D G D

D    D D G D D    D D G D    D    D D G D D    D D G D    D    D D G D D    D D G D

D    D D G D D    D D G D    D    D D G D D

# FLEXIBILITY

Velocity in high-register octaves. Practice at many different dynamic levels, and play with a tuner to keep the pitch accurate. Increase speed as possible.

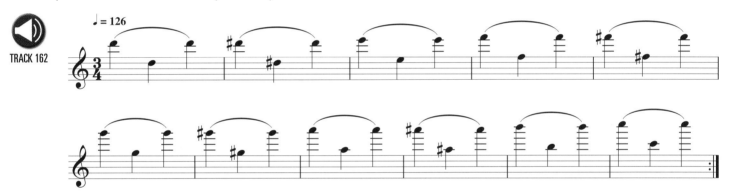

## TONE

High-register octaves. Keep your throat open and relaxed. Slower is better.

**TRACK 163**

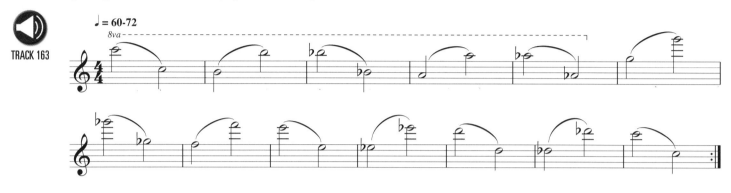

## SCALES

Full-range scales. Beginning on tonic, these scales go to the highest note in your range (high C or C#) and return to the lowest note in your range (low B or C) before returning to tonic. These should be played completely slurred. Increase speed as possible.

**TRACK 164**

C major, A♭ major, E major

## FINGER MOBILITY

Strive for evenness of fingers. Repeat each measure four times, more if necessary. Increase speed with the metronome over time. Transpose on the indicated starting pitches.

**TRACK 165**

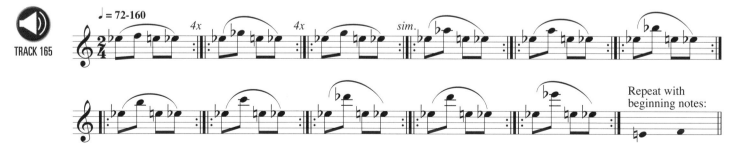

Repeat with beginning notes:

## ARTICULATION

Triple-tongue scales in thirds. Play through all major keys.

TRACK 166

## FLEXIBILITY

Concentrate on keeping the jaw open and relaxed throughout this study.

TRACK 167

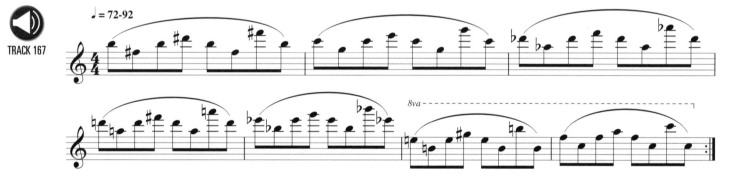

## TONE

High-register octaves. Let the bottom note spin into the upper note. Slower is better.

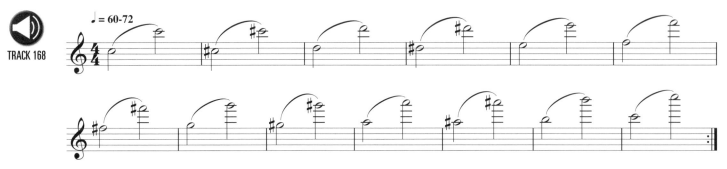

## SCALES

Full-range scales. Beginning on tonic, these scales go to the highest note in your range (high C or C♯) and return to the lowest note in your range (low B or C) before returning to tonic. These should be played completely slurred. Increase speed as possible. (See Track 164 for audio example.)

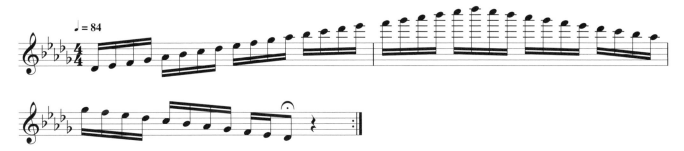

D♭ major, F major, A major

## FINGER MOBILITY

Strive for evenness of fingers. Repeat each measure four times, more if necessary. Increase speed with the metronome over time. Transpose on the indicated starting pitches.

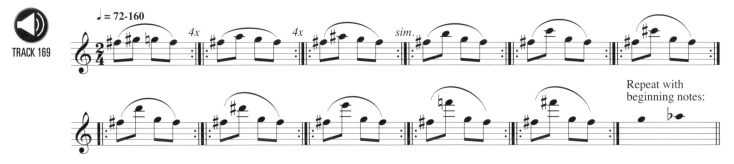

## ARTICULATION

Felix Mendelssohn, Symphony No. 4, movement 4. Triple-tongue study. Begin slowly to assure rhythmic accuracy. Be sure to count the rests carefully. When first learning this, try filling in the triplet rest with a played note. This will help solidify rhythm and improve accuracy.

**Note:** The audio track demonstrates measures 1–13 (beat 2).

TRACK 170

## FLEXIBILITY

Pitch-bending study. In the middle of each note, bend the pitch down as far as possible—using face, lips, and air—before returning to the pitch center. Pitch bending helps you find the core of your sound, in addition to building flexibility.

**Note:** The audio track demonstrates C, B, and B♭.

TRACK 171

# WEEK 41

## TONE

Johannes Brahms, Symphony No. 4, movement 4. This study focuses on fullness of tone. Play the excerpt very full—imagine you are a French horn player.

**TRACK 172**

## SCALES

Full-range scales. Beginning on tonic, these scales go to the highest note in your range (high C or C#) and return to the lowest note in your range (low B or C) before returning to tonic. These should be played completely slurred. Increase speed as possible. (See Track 164 for audio example.)

Gb major, Bb major, D major

## FINGER MOBILITY

Strive for evenness of fingers. Repeat each measure four times, more if necessary. Increase speed with the metronome over time. Transpose on the indicated starting pitches.

**TRACK 173**

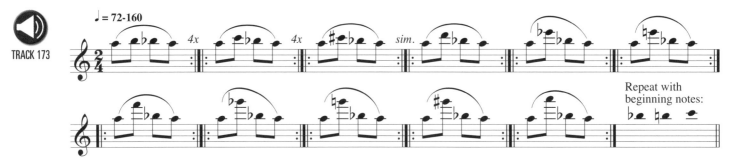

## ARTICULATION

Triple-tongue endurance. Play the following exercise on all your two-octave major and minor scales.

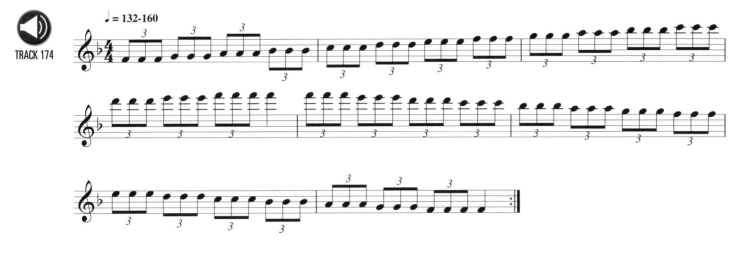

## FLEXIBILITY

Pitch-bending study. In the middle of each note, bend the pitch down as far as possible—using face, lips, and air—before returning to the pitch center. Pitch bending helps you find the core of your sound, in addition to building flexibility.

**Note:** The audio track demonstrates C major only.

Repeat the pattern, continuing with arpeggios that begin on the following notes:

## SCALES

Full-range scales. Beginning on tonic, these scales go to the highest note in your range (high C or C#) and return to the lowest note in your range (low B or C) before returning to tonic. These should be played completely slurred. Increase speed as possible. (See Track 164 for audio example.)

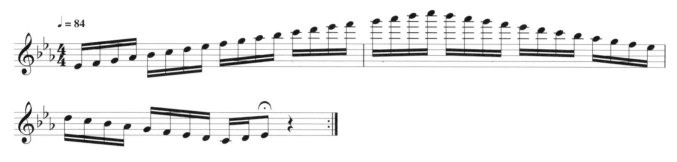

Eb major, B major, G major

## FINGER MOBILITY

Strive for evenness of fingers. Repeat each measure four times, more if necessary. Increase speed with the metronome over time. Transpose on the indicated starting pitches.

TRACK 176

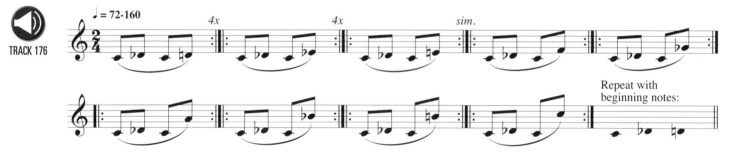

## FLEXIBILITY

Pitch bending in arpeggios. In this exercise, strive to begin and end the pitch-bended note with the same intonation. Practice with a tuner. Carefully place the fourth eighth note of each measure and return to that same pitch after the bend.

TRACK 177

# TONE AND ARTICULATION STUDY

W.A. Mozart, *Flute Concerto in G Major, K. 313*; movement 3. Focus on lightness of sound and clarity of articulation without clipping the slurred notes. You have two weeks for this study.

**Note:** The audio track demonstrates measures 1–20.

## SCALES (ARPEGGIOS)

Diminished, minor, major, augmented. Arpeggio studies are also fantastic tone exercises when played slowly. Begin these slowly, and work for seamless transitions between registers. Also, transpose beginning on C# and D.

**TRACK 179**

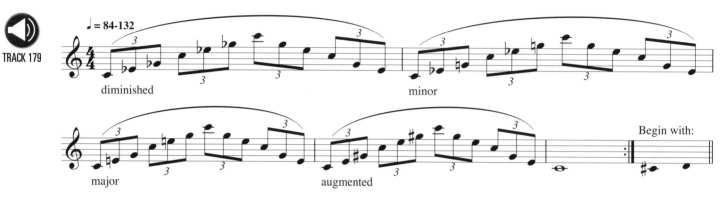

## FINGER MOBILITY

Strive for evenness of fingers. Repeat each measure four times, more if necessary. Increase speed with the metronome over time. Transpose on the indicated starting pitches.

**TRACK 180**

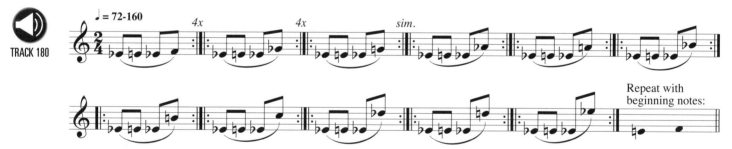

## FLEXIBILITY

Pitch bending in the high register. Play this with a tuner to ensure you don't start too high in pitch and that you return to the same place after the bend. This exercise is fantastic for developing flexibility to lower the pitch on all your high-register notes.

**TRACK 181**

# TONE AND ARTICULATION STUDY

W.A. Mozart, *Flute Concerto in G Major, K. 313*; movement 3. Continue to work on lightness of tone and accuracy of articulation while now increasing the tempo. (See Track 178 for audio example.)

## SCALES (ARPEGGIOS)

Diminished, minor, major, augmented. As you increase the speed, be thinking about which interval you need to raise as you go through the pattern. Staying one step ahead in your thoughts will increase the speed of your fingers. Transpose beginning on E and F. (See Track 179 for audio example.)

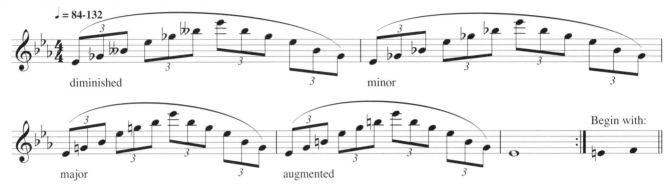

## FINGER MOBILITY

Strive for evenness of fingers. Repeat each measure four times, more if necessary. Increase speed with the metronome over time. Transpose on the indicated starting pitches.

TRACK 182

## TONE, FLEXIBILITY, AND ARTICULATION

Benjamin Godard, *Allegretto, Op. 116*. Strive for a wonderful combination of beautiful phrasing, scales, arpeggios, and articulations—all executed with flawless tone. Begin the technical passages slowly, assuring both even fingers and beautiful tone throughout. Remember that great technique can be lost if the tone isn't beautiful. You have two weeks for this study.

**Note:** The audio track demonstrates measures 1–27.

TRACK 183

## SCALES (ARPEGGIOS)

Diminished, minor, major, augmented. For a real challenge, use the drone function on your tuner. Set it to the tonic note of each scale and try to play all your octaves in tune with the tuner. Transpose beginning on G and G#. (See Track 179 for audio example.)

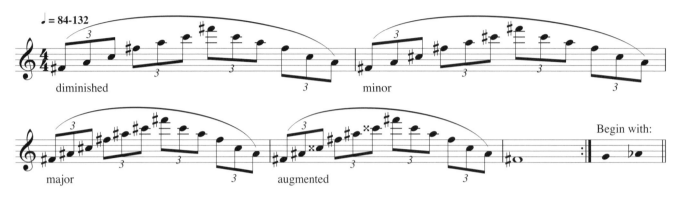

## FINGER MOBILITY

Strive for evenness of fingers. Repeat each measure four times, more if necessary. Increase speed with the metronome over time. Transpose on the indicated starting pitches.

TRACK 184

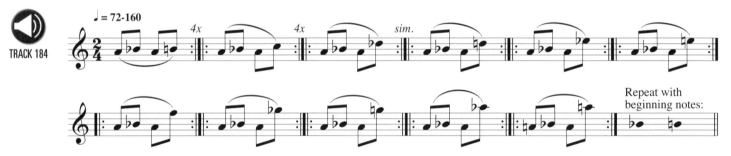

## TONE, FLEXIBILITY, AND ARTICULATION

Benjamin Godard, *Allegretto, Op. 116*. Continue to work on elegant phrasing, while now slowly increasing the tempo.

# WEEK 46

## SCALES (ARPEGGIOS)

Diminished, minor, major, augmented. Transpose beginning on B♭ and B. (See Track 179 for audio example.)

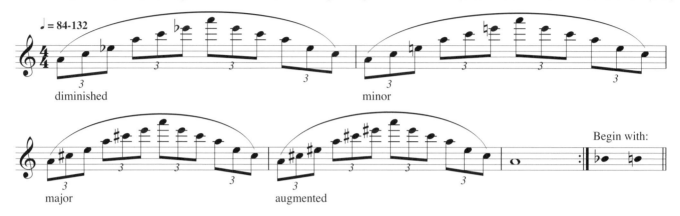

## FINGER MOBILITY

Strive for evenness of fingers. Repeat each measure four times, more if necessary. Increase speed with the metronome over time. Transpose on the indicated starting pitches.

TRACK 185

## TONE, FLEXIBILITY, AND ARTICULATION

J.S. Bach, *Partita in A Minor, BWV 1013*, movement 4. The tone challenge in this movement is different because the clarity and quality of tone must be maintained despite the technical nature of the movement. Bach's acrobatic writing notwithstanding, the piece must be beautiful throughout. Play close attention to the variety of articulations. You have two weeks for this exercise.

**Note:** The audio track demonstrates measures 1–20.

TRACK 186

# WEEK 47

## SCALES

Whole-tone scales. Whole tone scales are scales comprised entirely of whole steps. Because of that, there are only two whole tone scales, one beginning on C and the other on C#. That doesn't mean your options are limited. Try playing these beginning on any note to work on the theory behind the scale.
**Note:** The audio track demonstrates C only.

**TRACK 187**

## FINGER MOBILITY

Strive for evenness of fingers. Repeat each measure four times, more if necessary. Increase speed with the metronome over time. Transpose on the indicated starting pitches.

**TRACK 188**

## TONE, FLEXIBILITY, AND ARTICULATION

J.S. Bach, *Partita in A Minor, BWV 1013*, movement 4. By now you have likely worked out the technical challenges and it is time to return your attention to musical ideas. Remember to phrase—add your own dynamics and articulations, and be creative and flexible with your sense of time. Listen to lots of recordings for inspiration. (See Track 186 for audio example.)

# WEEK 48

## SCALES

Two-octave chromatic scales. Play these with a variety of articulations. Transpose up by half steps, through the full range of the flute.

**TRACK 189**

## FINGER MOBILITY

Strive for evenness of fingers. Repeat each measure four times, more if necessary. Increase speed with the metronome over time. Transpose on the indicated starting pitches.

**TRACK 190**

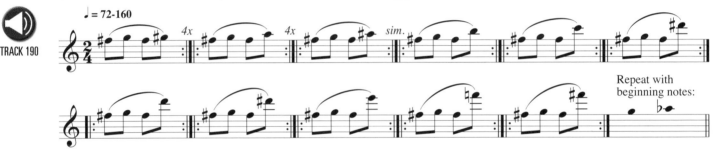

## TONE, FLEXIBILITY, AND ARTICULATION

Philippe Gaubert, *Madrigal*. Here's a beautiful, lush, melodic piece with sweeping scales and arpeggios. Your challenge is to execute them in a thoughtful, musical way. Be aware of your articulation choices. Remember the legato tongue. You have two weeks for this study.

**Note:** The audio track demonstrates measures 1–27 (beat 2).

**TRACK 191**

## SCALES

Full-range octatonic scales. Octatonic scales are comprised of alternating whole steps and half steps. For each tonic note, there are two variations of octatonic scales, one beginning with a whole step and one beginning with a half step. Play these beginning on any note, to work on the theory behind the scale.

TRACK 192

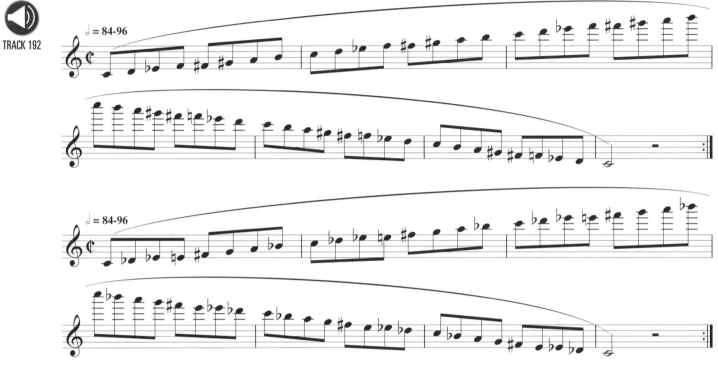

## FINGER MOBILITY

Strive for evenness of fingers. Repeat each measure four times, more if necessary. Increase speed with the metronome over time. Transpose on the indicated starting pitches.

TRACK 193

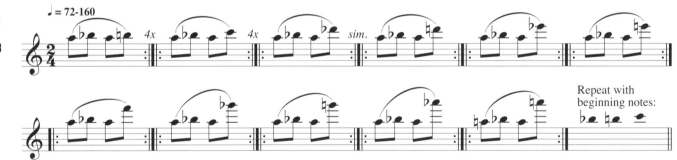

## TONE, FLEXIBILITY, AND ARTICULATION

Philippe Gaubert, *Madrigal*. This week, focus on beauty of sound throughout the movement. Experiment with different vowel shapes to create different tone colors, and use them to highlight your phrasing. (See Track 191 for audio example.)

# WEEK 50

## DIVERSIFIED EXPRESSION

Cécile Chaminade, *Concertino*. This piece offers a wonderful technical display of your skills. With beautiful singing melodies, sweeping scales, virtuosic playing, and a variety of articulations, the *Concertino* is a reward for all the technical studies!

TRACK 194

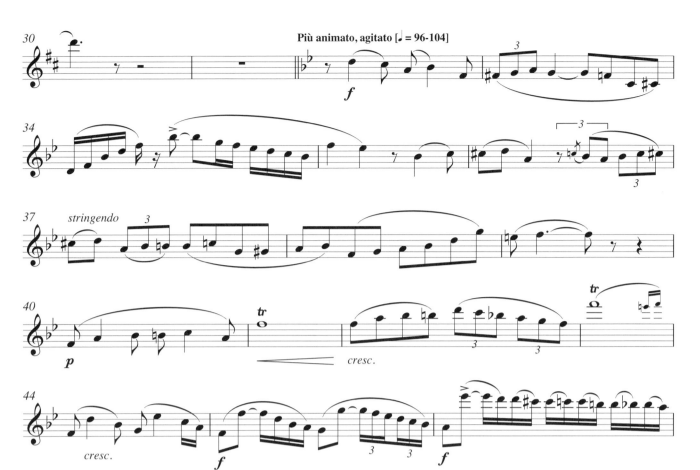

Più animato, agitato [♩ = 96-104]

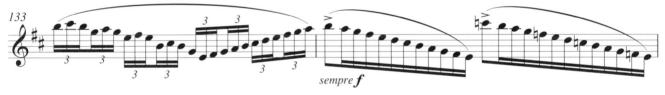

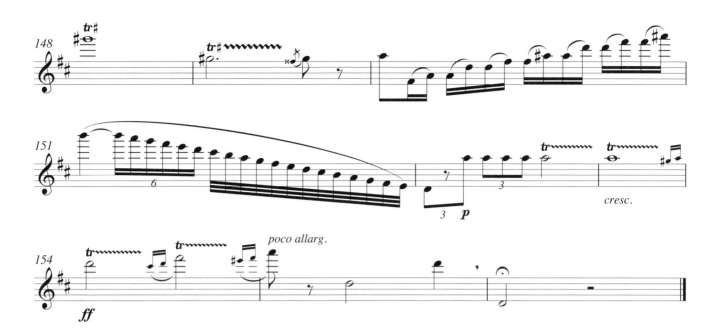

# ACKNOWLEDGMENTS

I would like to thank my editor, J. Mark Baker, for his patience with me on this project; my husband Tom and our three boys for tolerating my late nights and for their overwhelming enthusiasm for this undertaking; and my fellow Quintet Attacca members for entertaining my endless chat about this book. I'd also like to thank several notable teachers, without whom I would not be where I am today: Cynthia Stevens, Robert Goodberg, Donald Peck, and Walfrid Kujala.

# ABOUT THE AUTHOR

**Jennifer Clippert** began her musical career on the piccolo at age nine, and was forced to switch to the flute a few years later when she got braces on her teeth. Her infatuation with the instrument led to a life-long pursuit of perfection that continues today.

Ms. Clippert's performance career reflects her passionate knowledge of music from the Baroque to the present day. Equally comfortable as a soloist, chamber musician, and orchestral player, she has performed with many groups—such as the Chicago Symphony Orchestra, Grant Park Orchestra, Chicago Philharmonic, Music of the Baroque, the Chicago Symphony's MUSICNOW series, and Milwaukee's Present Music, among others. She has had the privilege of playing under many of today's prominent conductors, including Daniel Barenboim, Pierre Boulez, Sir Andrew Davis, Christoph Eschenbach, Lorin Maazel, Zubin Mehta, Kent Nagano, David Robertson, Sir Georg Solti, Robert Spano, John Williams, and Pinchas Zukerman. Her woodwind ensemble, Quintet Attacca, won both the Senior Wind Division and the Grand Prize at the Fischoff National Chamber Music Festival and has maintained an active performance schedule throughout the United States and abroad.

A graduate of the University of Wisconsin-Milwaukee, Ms. Clippert received her BFA in Flute Performance with Robert Goodberg. She also attended Northwestern University, where she received both her MM and DM degrees with Walfrid Kujala. She is currently Assistant Professor of Flute at the University of Wisconsin-Milwaukee.

# EXCEPTIONAL FLUTE PUBLICATIONS from HAL LEONARD

## BIG BOOK OF FLUTE SONGS

Flutists will love this giant collection of 130 popular solos! Includes: Another One Bites the Dust • Any Dream Will Do • Bad Day • Beauty and the Beast • Breaking Free • Clocks • Edelweiss • God Bless the U.S.A. • Heart and Soul • I Will Remember You • Imagine • Na Na Hey Hey Kiss Him Goodbye • Satin Doll • United We Stand • You Raise Me Up • and dozens more!
00842207   $14.95

## CLAUDE BOLLING – SUITE FOR FLUTE AND JAZZ PIANO TRIO

This suite in seven parts is composed for a "classic" flute and a "jazz" piano. It was the first jazz recording of world-renowned flutist Jean-Pierre Rampal and Claude Bolling. It is possible to play the whole piece with only flute and piano, but bass and drum parts are included for the complete Suite. The CD includes full recordings and flute play-along tracks for seven songs: Baroque and Blue • Fugace • Irlandaise • Javanaise • Sentimentale • Veloce • Versatile.
00672558   Set of Parts/CD   $59.95

## THE BOOSEY & HAWKES FLUTE ANTHOLOGY

24 PIECES BY 16 COMPOSERS

*Boosey & Hawkes*

Intermediate to advanced literature from the Romantic era to the 20th century. Special study paid to various state high school contest solo repertory lists. Contents: Gavotte and Musette from Divertimento (Alwyn) • Scherzo from Suite Paysanne Hongroise (Bartók) • First Movement from Duo for Flute and Piano (Copland) • Vocalise (Copland) • Valentine Piece, Op. 70 (Górecki) • Duo for Two Flutes (Lees) • Rhapsody on a Theme of Paganini, Op. 43 (Rachmaninoff) • and many more.
48019634   $24.99

## FLUTE FINGERING CHART

FOR FLUTE AND PICCOLO

*Music Sales America*

In addition to a detailed fingering chart, this handy laminated fold-out card includes notes about instrument care, transposition, pitch system, and notation. A valuable tool for any flute player!
14011341   $7.95

## THE G. SCHIRMER FLUTE ANTHOLOGY

14 WORKS FROM THE 20TH CENTURY

*G. Schirmer, Inc.*

Selected works from the most prominent G. Schirmer and AMP composers, including music by Barber, Corigliano, Harbison, Martinu, Moyse, Muczynski, and others. With detailed notes on the music. Suitable for the advanced high school and college level player. Includes works for solo flute as well as flute and piano.
50499531   $19.99

## IMPROVISATION FOR FLUTE

THE SCALE/MODE APPROACH

*by Andy McGhee*

*Berklee Press*

Expand the creative breadth of your soloing! The step-by-step exercises and explanations in this tried-&-true resource will help you develop your ear and improve your technique. You'll learn the intimate relationships between modes and chords, practicing licks and solos that grow out of their underlying harmonies and sound natural.
50449810   $14.99

## JAZZ FLUTE ETUDES

*Houston Publishing, Inc.*

These etudes by Marc Adler will delight both classical and jazz musicians. Marc is an accomplished flutist and composer in both the jazz and classical arenas and is also an experienced educator. These twelve etudes explore each of the twelve keys but at the same time step out into contemporary sounds characteristic of modern jazz and 20th-century classical music, such as whole tone and diminished scales, and colorful chord progressions. Jazz flutists will enjoy his original jazz licks and may want to add some of them to their vocabulary of patterns.
00030442   $12.95

## JETHRO TULL – FLUTE SOLOS

AS PERFORMED BY IAN ANDERSON

*transcribed by Jeff Rona*

Flute solos from 18 Jethro Tull songs have been transcribed for this collection. Songs include: Bungle in the Jungle • Cross-Eyed Mary • Fire at Midnight • Look into the Sun • Nothing Is Easy • Thick as a Brick • The Witch's Promise • and more.
00672547   $12.99

## MELODIOUS AND PROGRESSIVE STUDIES FOR FLUTE

*compiled and revised by Robert Cavally*

For many years Robert Cavally's *Melodious and Progressive Studies* has been one of the most important series for intermediate flute study. Book 1 contains a wealth of famous studies by such composers as Andersen, Gariboldi, Köhler and Terschak. Book 2 is a continuation of Book 1 and also includes etudes by Kummer. For further technical and musical development, Book 3 features the work of Boehm, Kronke, Köhler and Mollerup, as well as excerpts of solos by Haydn, Bizet, LeClair and Jongen.
00970024   Book 1         $13.99
00970025   Book 2         $13.99
00970031   Book 3         $12.99
00970012   Book 4A        $14.95
00970013   Book 4B        $13.50

## 101 FLUTE TIPS

STUFF ALL THE PROS KNOW AND USE

*by Elaine Schmidt*

Tips, suggestions, advice and other useful information garnered through a lifetime of flute study and professional gigging are all presented in this book with dozens of entries gleaned from first-hand experience. Topics covered include: selecting the right flute for you • finding the right teacher • warm-up exercises • practicing effectively • taking good care of your flute • gigging advice • staying and playing healthy • members of the flute family • extended ranges and techniques • and flute fraternization.
00119883   Book/CD Pack   $14.99

## HAL•LEONARD® CORPORATION

7777 W. BLUEMOUND RD. P.O. BOX 13819 MILWAUKEE, WI 53213